SUMMER SMART

Grade

4 • 5

Special thanks are given to
Vikalp Jain**, **Dev Patel**, **Tiffany Feler**, **Erica Ho**, and **Marco Chang
for their involvement in the Arts & Crafts Section.

Printed in China

Contents

Grade 4–5

Mathematics

Social Studies

Arts & Crafts

A. **See how much the children spent on the food. Write the amount and food items in the boxes. Then answer the questions.**

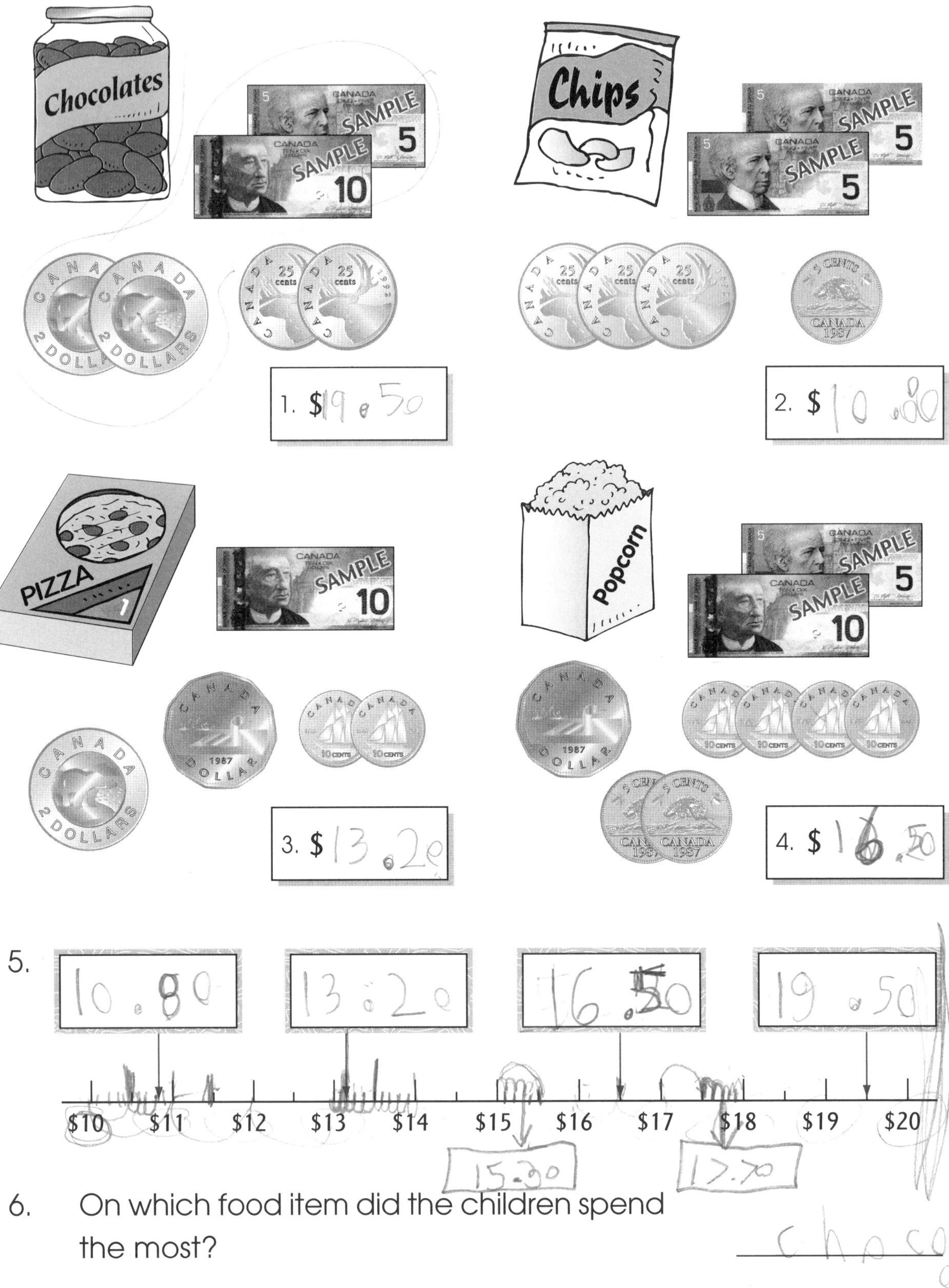

6. On which food item did the children spend the most? ____________

7. How much did the children spend on chocolates and chips? ____________

8. How much did the children spend in all? ____________

B. Look at the pictures and complete the sentences.

1. The cake is divided equally into 8 pieces, with each piece weighing ________ g. 5 pieces of the cake weigh ________ g in all.

2. 

The bottle holds ________ mL of orange juice. If Ray drinks 550 mL of orange juice, there will be ________ mL of orange juice left.

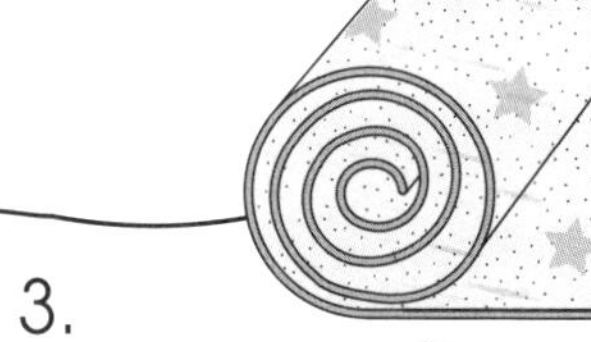

3.
   a. Each roll of roll-up candy is 40 cm, or ________ mm long.
   b. 3 rolls of roll-up candy have a length of ________ cm.
   c. ________ rolls of roll-up candy have a length of 2 m.

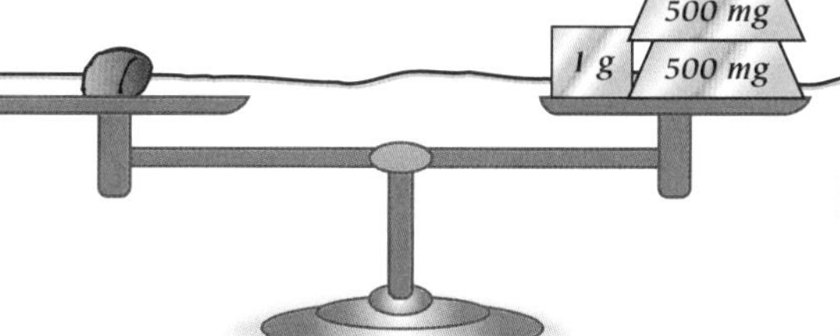

4.
   a. A marshmallow weighs ________ g or ________ mg.
   b. A bag of 100 marshmallows weighs ________ g.
   c. A bag of 1000 marshmallows weighs ________ g or ________ kg.

C. **Write the children's names on the lines to show how much food they ate. Then complete the sentences.**

1. Henry ate $\frac{1}{8}$ of a cake, Ray ate $\frac{3}{8}$, and Elaine ate $\frac{2}{8}$.

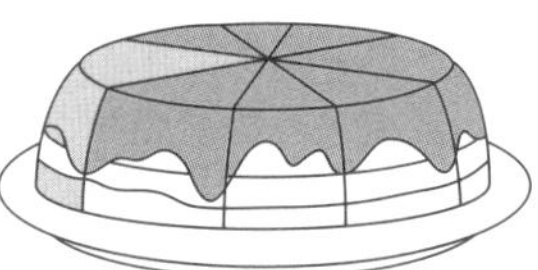 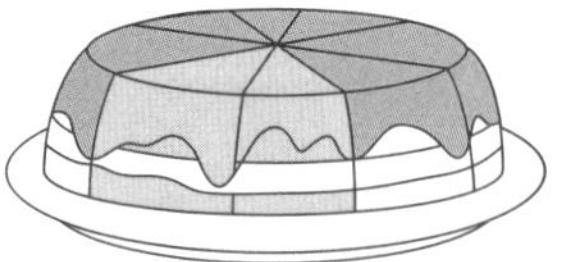 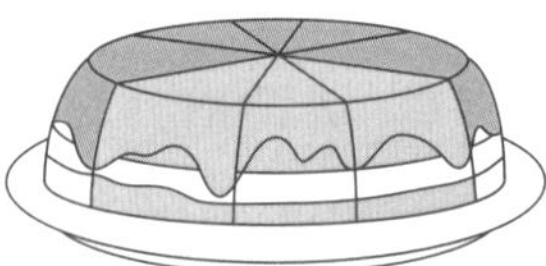

a. ____________ b. ____________ c. ____________

d. ____________ ate the most; ____________ ate the least.

2. Tim ate $\frac{3}{10}$ of a box of chocolates, David ate 0.5, and Suzy ate 0.2.

a. ____________ b. ____________ c. ____________

d. ____________ ate the most; ____________ ate the least.

3. Alex ate $1\frac{1}{4}$ oranges, Gloria ate $\frac{3}{4}$, and Sean ate $1\frac{2}{4}$.

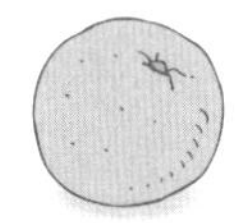  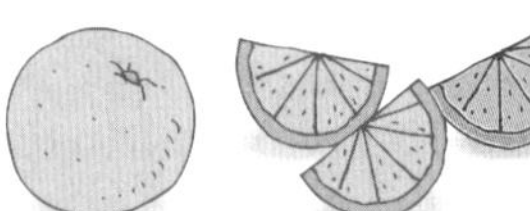  

a. ____________ b. ____________ c. ____________

d. ____________ ate the most; ____________ ate the least.

D. Read what the children say. Help them solve the problems.

1. *2 bottles each containing 725 mL of cola can fill 3 glasses. If I drink 3 glasses of cola, how many millilitres of cola do I drink?*

________ mL of cola

2. 

I bought 818 g of gumdrops. I keep 126 g for myself and divide the rest among 4 friends. How many grams of gumdrops does each of my friends get?

________ g of gumdrops

3. *1599 lollipops are packed into packets of 7 or 8 lollipops. If there are 115 packets of 8 lollipops, how many packets of 7 lollipops are there?*

________ packets of 7 lollipops

each

Help Jonathan solve the problem.

I bought 80 lollipops at 15¢ each. If each lollipop cost 5¢ more, how many fewer lollipops could I buy with the same amount of money?

Jonathan could buy ________ fewer lollipops.

Thousands of people, young and old, stand silently and watch as Tiger Woods steps up to the first tee. Tiger takes one look at his target and methodically adjusts his grip and his feet. He raises his club and makes the ideal swing. The crowd explodes into a cheer as the golf ball soars through the air and lands directly in the middle of the fairway. Another perfect shot for Tiger.

Eldrick "Tiger" Woods was born on December 30, 1975. At the age of six months, Tiger watched as his father hit golf balls into a net. By the age of 11 months, he began swinging his own miniature club. This was the beginning of what has turned out to be a sensational golf career.

At the age of 21, Tiger joined the pro tour. During that year, he won two Professional Golf Association (PGA) tour events and ended the year winning a total of $790 594. He continues to be one of the all time leading money earners in professional sport.

Apart from his obvious athletic ability, Tiger Woods also possesses many qualities that make him a dominating force in the world of golf. He is disciplined and focused, and perseveres through challenging situations. Tiger constantly works to improve his game. Despite the flashes of cameras and the roar of the crowd, he continues to maintain his concentration. Throughout his career, Tiger has had to deal with criticism and injury, but his positive attitude sees him through these experiences. Tiger Woods has become a hero and role model for thousands of young people around the world.

A. Write "T" for the true sentences and "F" for the false ones.

1. ______ Tiger Woods is a famous golfer.
2. ______ Tiger was 11 years of age when he started to swing a club.
3. ______ He does not practise on a regular basis.
4. ______ Tiger Woods is a role model for young golfers.
5. ______ Tiger Woods has remained healthy all his career.
6. ______ "Tiger" is a nickname.

B. Find sentences in the story to show that Tiger Woods:

1. enjoyed the game of golf at a very young age.

   ____

2. is rarely affected by negative events.

   ____

3. stays very focused when he is in a game.

   ____

4. has qualities that make him a great golfer.

   ____

5. performed very well as a young golfer.

   ____

   ____

C. **Read the clues and complete the crossword puzzle with words from the passage.**

Across

A. controlling
B. negative comment
C. small
D. demanding
E. keep

Down

1. orderly
2. spectacular
3. perfect

Week 1 ENGLISH

D. Place the proper punctuation at the end of each sentence.

Write "T" for telling sentences.
Write "A" for asking sentences.
Write "E" for exclamatory sentences.
Write "I" for imperative sentences.

1. How far did the golf ball travel ______
2. Tiger Woods has an excellent swing ______
3. Pick up the tee ______
4. Watch out ______
5. What a shot ______

E. You have been chosen to interview Tiger Woods. Make a list of questions you would like to ask him.

Begin with a few direct questions about basic factual information (e.g. How many hours a day do you practise?).

1. ____________________
2. ____________________

Next, ask more detailed questions (e.g. Who is your hero?).

3. ____________________
4. ____________________

Finally, move to open-ended questions that draw out Tiger's experiences and opinions (e.g. Can you describe the most thrilling moment of your career?).

5. ____________________
6. ____________________

Week 1

SCIENCE

A. Identify the animals that display the adaptation. Write their names on the lines.

wood frog

polar bear

viceroy butterfly

beaver

wolf

white fox

preying mantis

1. This mammal's front teeth continue to grow throughout its entire life.

   ____

2. This insect's camouflage is used to hide itself from prey.

   ____

3. This winged copycat does not taste bad…but looks like a relative that does!

   ____

4. This Arctic amphibian freezes solid in the winter and thaws out in the spring.

   ____

5. This huge, white appearing mammal's hair is actually translucent (see-through) so it can reflect heat from the sun down to its black skin!

   ____

6. When this animal hunts for food, it does not hunt alone!

   ____

7. This Arctic sly one has a small muzzle and ears when compared to its southerly red relative.

   ____

B. Rebecca has taken some pictures of how certain birds have beaks and feet that are adapted to the lives that they lead. Help her match the proper note with each photo. Write the letter.

designed for perching, this claw is sure to keep its owner secure on twigs (1)

...just like a straw that you'd see in a milkshake...this one sips! (2)

...tearing flesh is the main job here (3)

...it uses its beak to crack the shells of seeds to reach the nutritious interior that makes up his diet... (4)

...you can really see how we have copied nature's design here...scuba divers should thank the ducks! (5)

the power in these claws must be great to hold on to its supper (6)

A. **The map below shows the landform regions of Canada. Label the various regions.**

Innuitian Region Interior Plains Hudson Bay Lowlands
Canadian Shield Arctic Lowlands Cordilleran Region
Appalachian Region St. Lawrence Lowlands

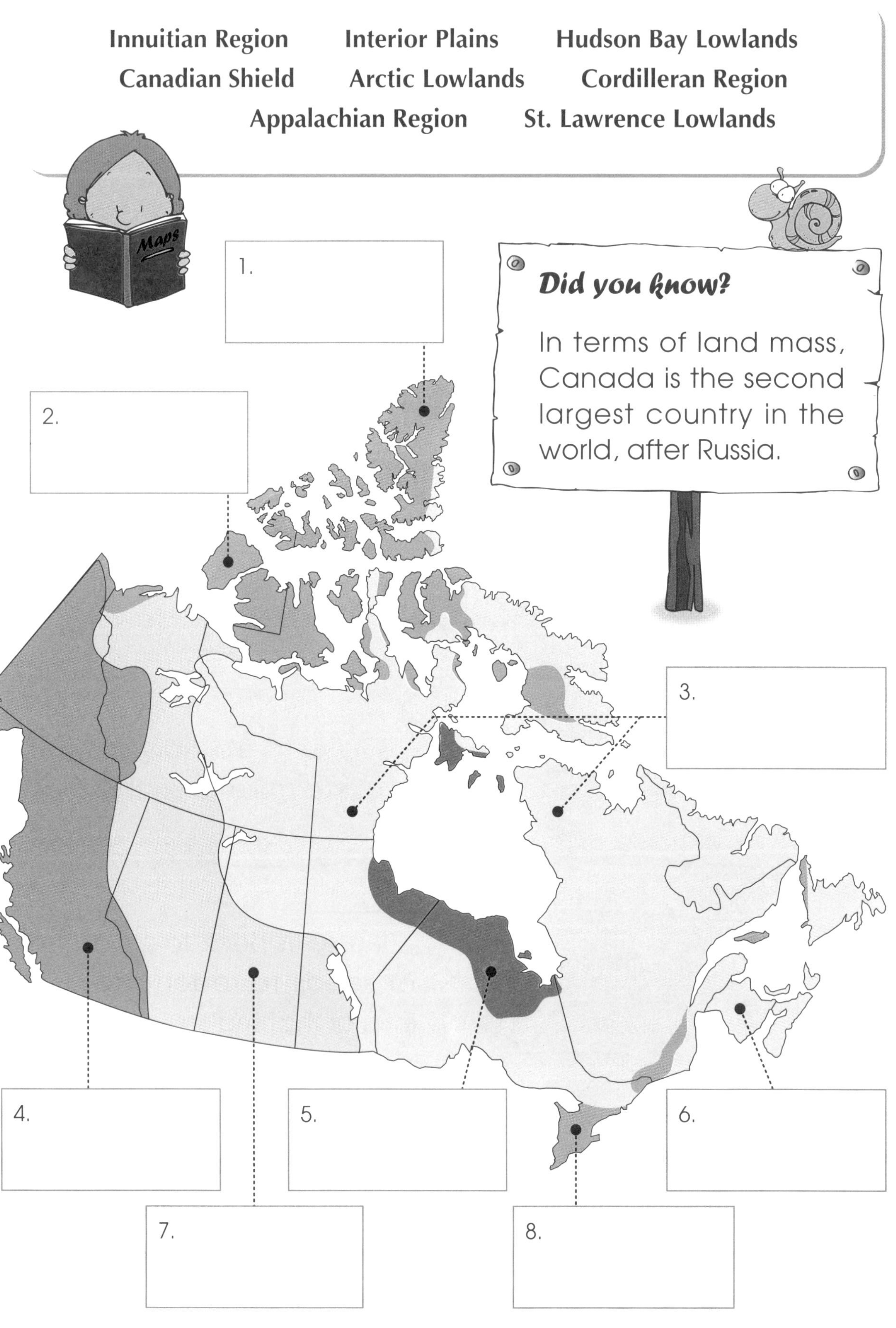

Did you know?

In terms of land mass, Canada is the second largest country in the world, after Russia.

B. Circle the correct answer for each statement below.

1. There are ___ mountain regions in Canada.

   A. one B. two C. three

2. The Appalachian Region includes ___ and the four Atlantic provinces.

   A. Ontario B. Quebec C. British Columbia

3. Copper, lead, silver, gold, and zinc are mined in ___ .

   A. Western Cordillera B. Arctic Lowlands
   C. St. Lawrence Lowlands

4. More than half of Canada is part of the ___ .

   A. Cordilleran Region B. Interior Plains
   C. Canadian Shield

5. The ___ covers parts of Alberta, Saskatchewan, and Manitoba.

   A. Interior Plains B. Appalachian Region
   C. Hudson Bay Lowlands

6. Salmon, herring, shellfish, and halibut are natural resources in ___ .

   A. Western Cordillera B. St. Lawrence Lowlands
   C. Appalachian Region

Challenge

1. How many lakes are there in Canada?

   A. about 20 000 B. about 200 000 C. about 2 000 000

2. Name the five Great Lakes.

   ____

   ____

Week

1

ARTS & CRAFTS

Calypso Coasters

MATERIALS:

- sealer
- scissors
- paintbrush
- foam sheets
- bright-coloured paint
- pencil or pen for tracing
- small plastic lid from yogurt or margarine container

DIRECTIONS:

1. Using lid as tracer, trace 6 circles per set of coasters. Cut out.

2. Give each coaster a base coat of paint. Let dry.

3. Paint geometric designs using bright colours.

4. "Paint" with sealer.

A. Susan walked her dog along the trail. Help her write the distance she travelled as decimals in kilometres.

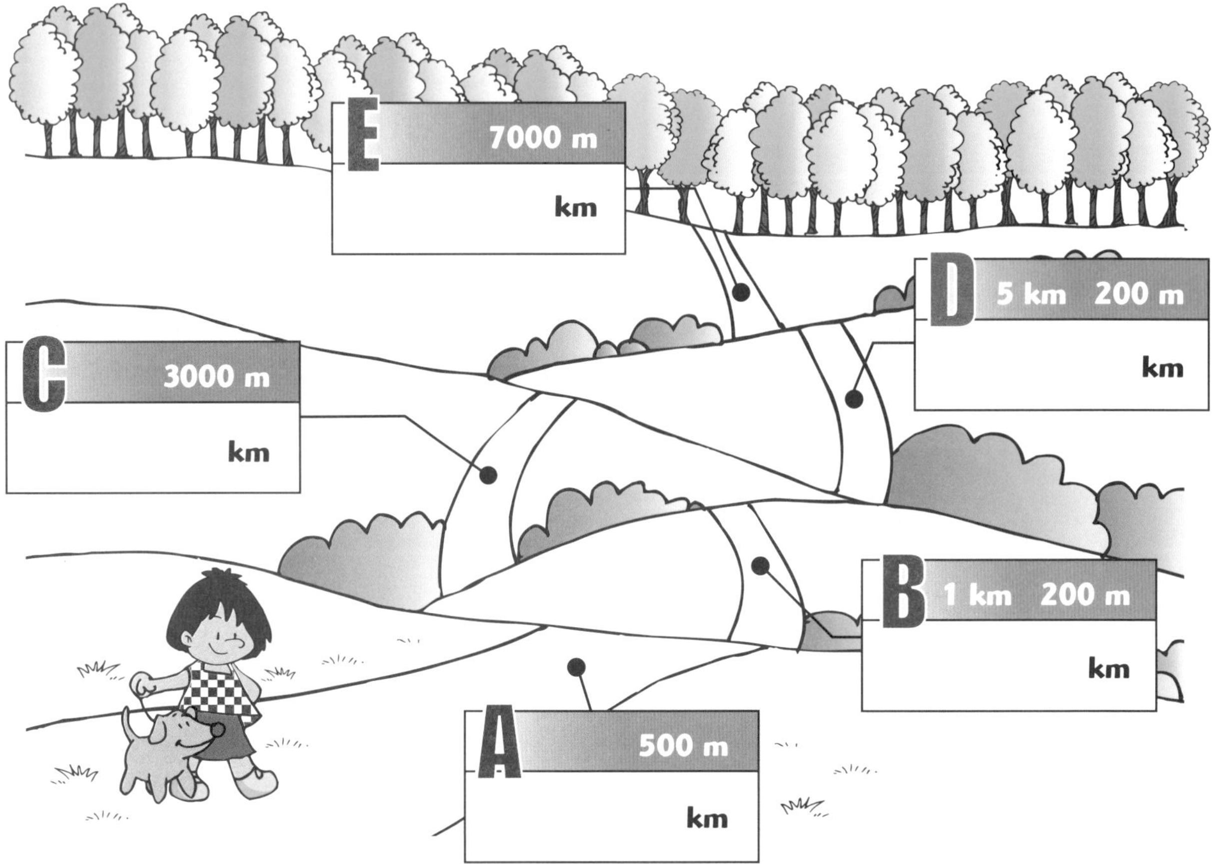

B. Help Susan find her travelling times.

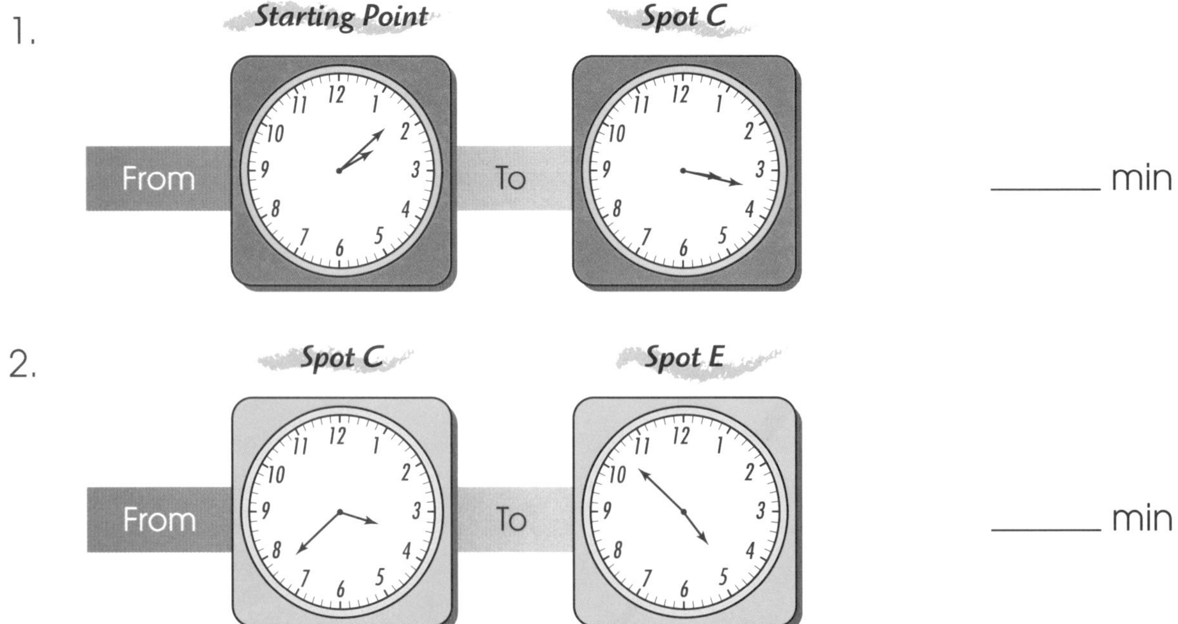

1. ______ min

2. ______ min

3. The total time it took Susan to walk along the trail was ______ min, or ______ h ______ min.

C. Susan saw a lot of things along the trail. Look at the pictures. Help Susan complete the sentences with decimals and fractions.

1. 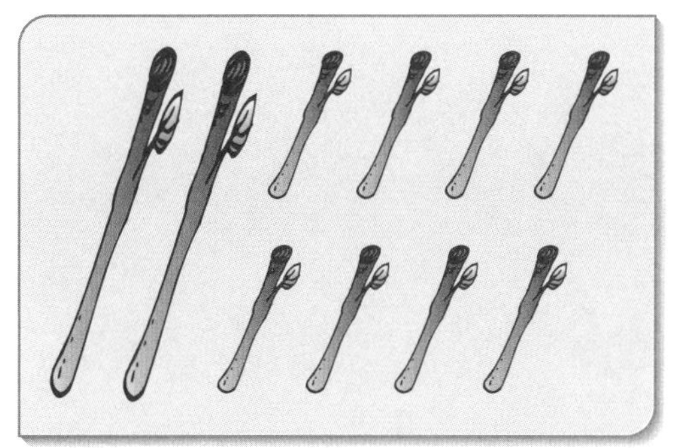

0.2 or $\frac{\quad}{10}$ of the sticks were long.

______ or ______ of the sticks were short.

2. 

______ or ______ of the flowers had 5 petals.

______ or ______ of the flowers had 8 petals.

3. 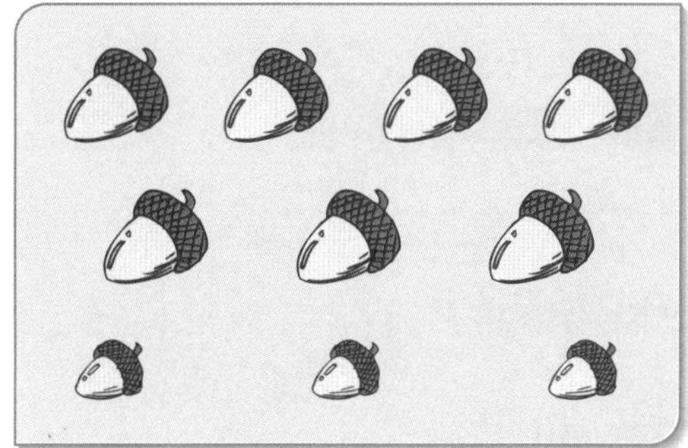

______ or ______ of the acorns were big.

______ or ______ of the acorns were small.

4. 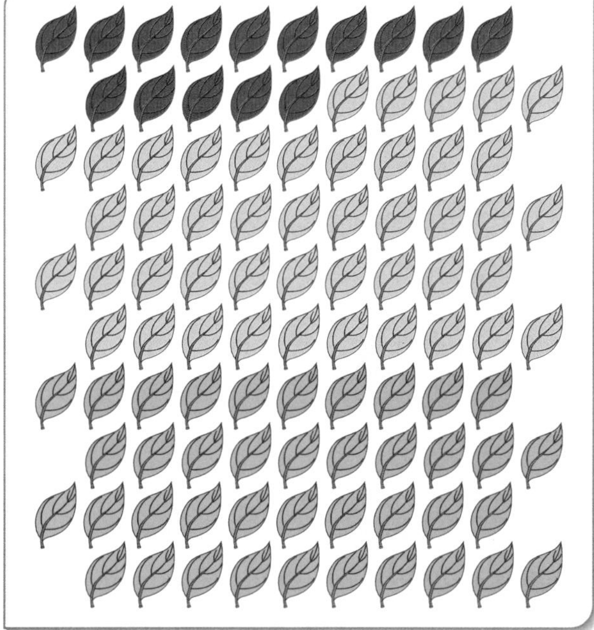

______ or ______ of the leaves were red.

______ or ______ of the leaves were yellow.

______ or ______ of the leaves were green.

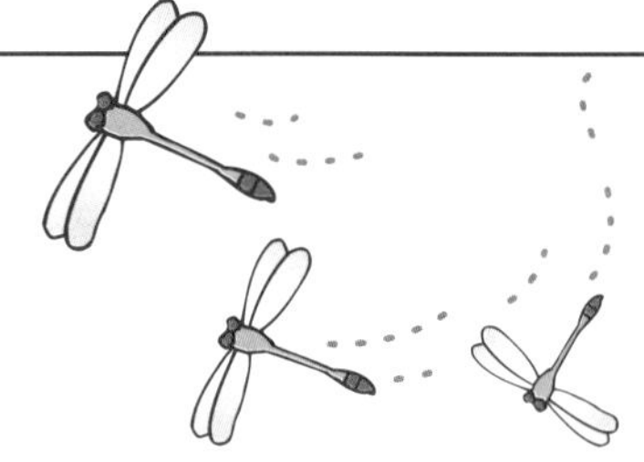

D. **Help Susan measure and record the length of each blade of grass to the nearest millimetre. Then solve the problems.**

1. (A)

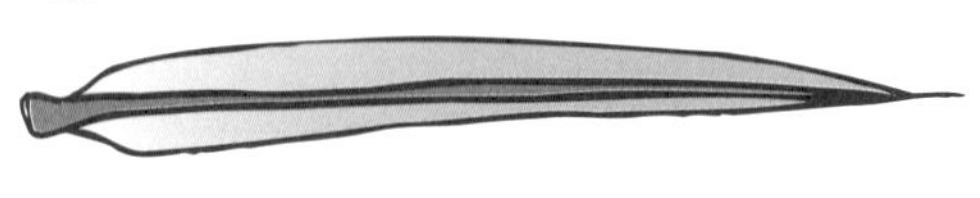

____ mm

2. (B)

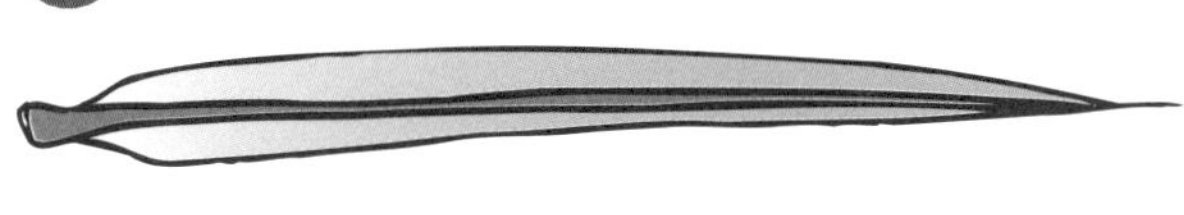

____ mm

3. (C)

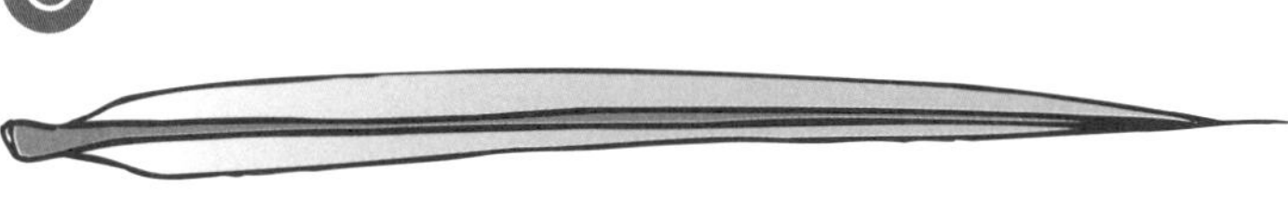

____ mm

4. (D)

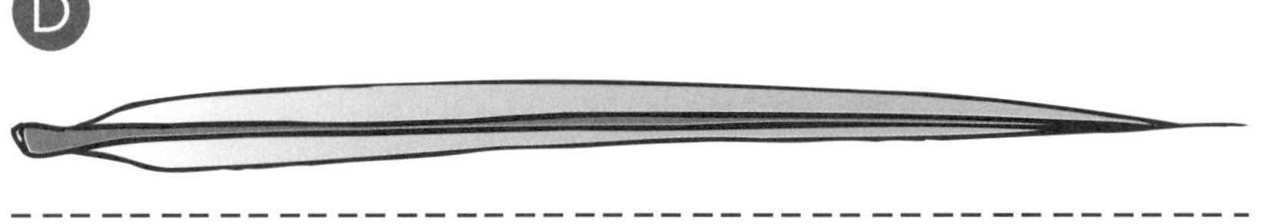

____ mm

5. What is the length of (B) in centimetres? ____ cm

6. What is the length of (D) in centimetres? ____ cm

7. Susan followed a pattern to display the grass. What is the pattern?

____

8. To continue the pattern, what is the length of the next blade of grass? ____ mm

9. If Susan uses 100 blades of grass each 92 mm long to weave a grass necklace, what will the total length of the grass be? ____ cm

Week 2

MATHEMATICS

E. Help Susan choose the best estimation. Circle the correct answers.

1. The height of a tree

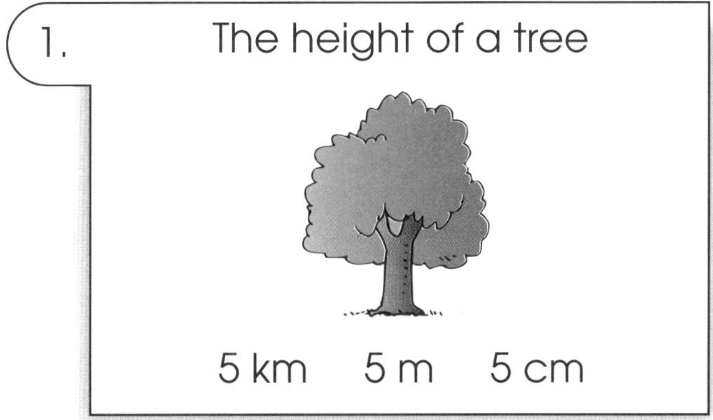

5 km 5 m 5 cm

2. The perimeter of a leaf

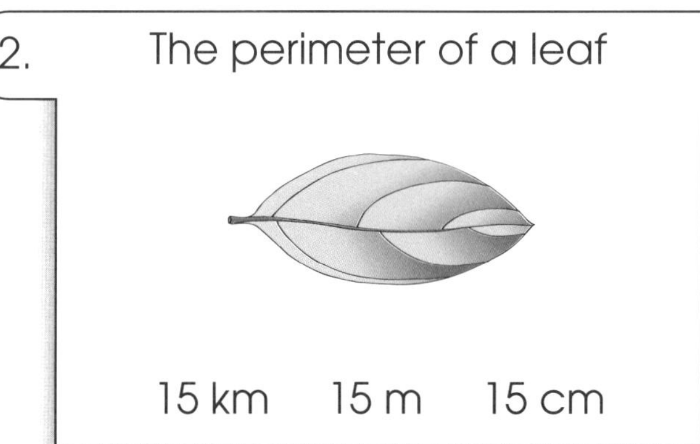

15 km 15 m 15 cm

3. The area of a pond

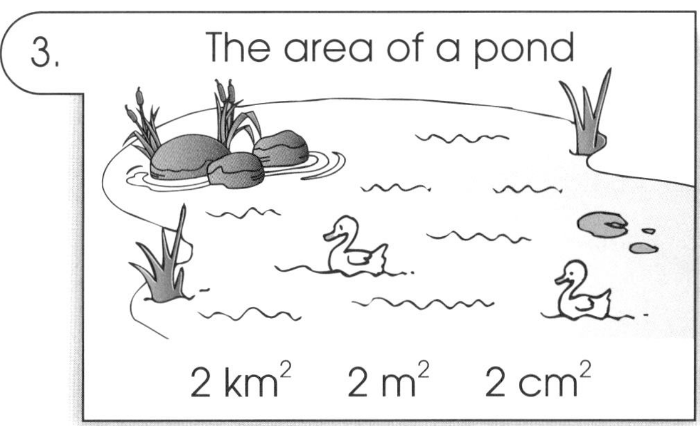

$2\ km^2$ $2\ m^2$ $2\ cm^2$

4. The area of the shadow of a tree

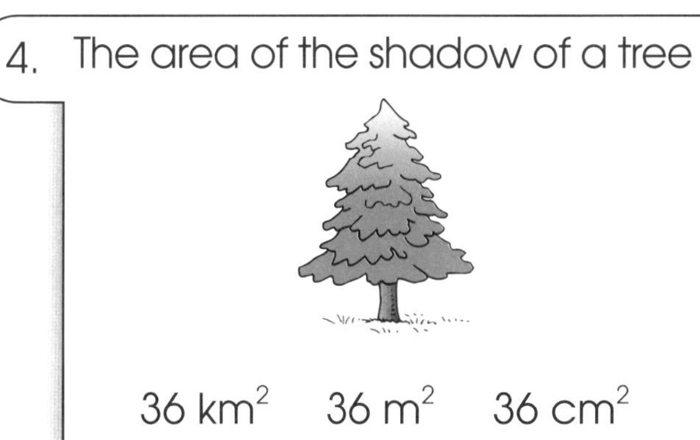

$36\ km^2$ $36\ m^2$ $36\ cm^2$

Help Little Squirrel find the path to his food. Join the dots in order from the least value to the greatest.

Kayak

The kayak is a watercraft that was created by the Inuit of the North thousands of years ago. This form of transportation continues to be used today. A kayak is a light boat that is propelled by a double-bladed paddle.

Historically, the frame of the kayak was made from driftwood and whalebones. Animal skins were then stretched over this frame. Kayaks were mainly used on hunting expeditions for caribou and seals. They ranged in width depending on what size of animal was being hunted and the length of the journey. A wider kayak was usually used for long journeys. It could hold large game and up to two people. Kayaks of the past were very sensitive to weather conditions. The skins would easily lose their shape and the frame would crack when the temperature and humidity changed.

Today, kayaks are mainly used for recreation and sport. They are made from fibreglass or strong plastics. Partitions, leg braces, and footrests have been added to improve the strength of the construction. Competitive athletes like the design of modern kayaks because they are comfortable and feel like an extension of their body. The heavy construction of present-day kayaks allows the paddler to travel skilfully through white water rapids and perform underwater rolls and dives.

The design and the construction of the kayak have met the needs of the people of the past and present. This manoeuvrable water vehicle continues to be popular with paddling enthusiasts.

A. The following scrambled words are from the reading passage. Use the definition to help unscramble each.

1. ptanttrrnosaio – the act of carrying people or goods

   ___ ___ ___ ___ ___ ___ ___ ___ ___ ___ ___ ___ ___ ___

2. pextisideno – trips made for special purposes

   ___ ___ ___ ___ ___ ___ ___ ___ ___ ___ ___

3. ntcornucisto – the building of something

   ___ ___ ___ ___ ___ ___ ___ ___ ___ ___ ___ ___

4. eintsisve – easily affected by outside factors

   ___ ___ ___ ___ ___ ___ ___ ___ ___

5. ncerarteio – a relaxing activity

   ___ ___ ___ ___ ___ ___ ___ ___ ___ ___

B. Using information from the passage, complete the following chart.

Kayaks of the	***Past***	***Present***
Design		
Uses		

C. **Match the present tense verbs with the past tense verbs. Write the verbs on the lines.**

1. ____________ wear
2. ____________ find
3. ____________ drink
4. ____________ ride
5. ____________ run
6. ____________ give
7. ____________ sing
8. ____________ break
9. ____________ draw
10. ____________ buy

PAST TENSE

drank
sang
ran
drew
wore
rode
gave
found
broke
bought

D. **Use the past tense verbs in (C) to complete the sentences below.**

1. I ____________ in a kayak on Lake Ontario.
2. We ____________ a surprise gift for our cousin.
3. She ____________ me a lesson on how to paddle a kayak.
4. The dog ____________ my mom's favourite vase.
5. The explorers ____________ the pieces of an old canoe.
6. I ____________ a lifejacket when kayaking.
7. They ____________ to the shore to meet the hunter.
8. We ____________ and danced around the camp fire.
9. The children ____________ cold water after the race.
10. She ____________ a sketch of me and gave it to me as my birthday present.

E. Proofread the following paragraph. Underline the misspelled words and rewrite them on the lines below.

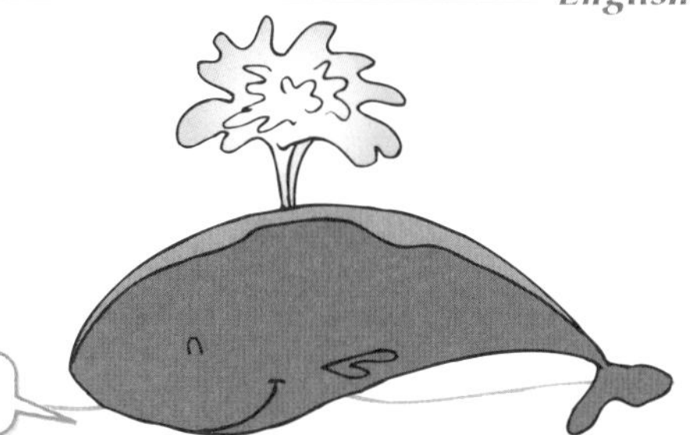

Hello!

Last summor, I travelled to Newfoundland with my family. While their, we went kayaking in the Atlantic Ocean. I couldn't beleive my eyes when a large whale approched our kayaks. At first I was afraid that the whale mite flip us over with it's strong tail. I was wrong. The whale just came to say hello.

____

____

F. In each paragraph below, put a line through the sentence that does not belong.

1. To the competitive athlete, the kayak is like an extension of their body. They sit snugly in it and with their outstanding skills, they can travel through white water rapids with ease and even perform underwater rolls and dives. Before we go kayaking, we have to put on lifejackets and other protective gear. This, of course, calls for years of intensive training.

2. Soccer is growing in popularity in North America. Unlike American football, soccer players are not allowed to touch the ball with their hands, except, of course, the goalkeepers. Neither is body check allowed. The next World Cup series will be in 2010. So, players have to rely on their skills in controlling the ball with their feet.

Week 2

SCIENCE

A. Write the name of the animal that belongs in each verse.

bald eagle

I am a 1. ____________
From the sky I can see
The fish to bring back
To my nest in a tree.

I am a 2. ____________
I live underground
In forests and meadows
Where my supper is found.

I am a 3. ____________
Of trees I am fond
They're my shelter, my food
My dam for my pond.

I am a 4. ____________
I need to keep moist
Under rocks, under logs
Underneath is my choice.

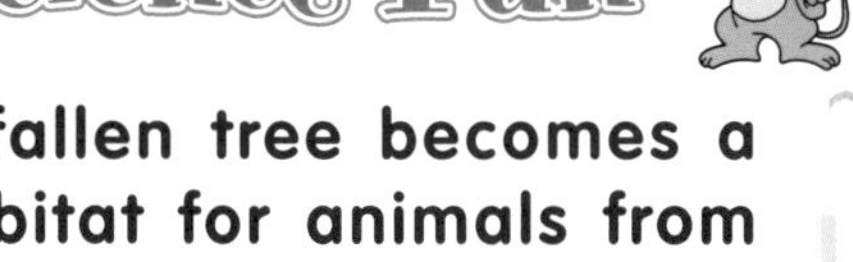

A fallen tree becomes a habitat for animals from insects to deer, providing food and shelter.

Many people around the world are helping to protect the world's habitats. This biologist has been making observations about animals and their habitats.

B. List the names of the observed animals in the proper places.

Except for its nesting grounds, an albatross's habitat is entirely at sea.

Animal Habitats and Their Animals

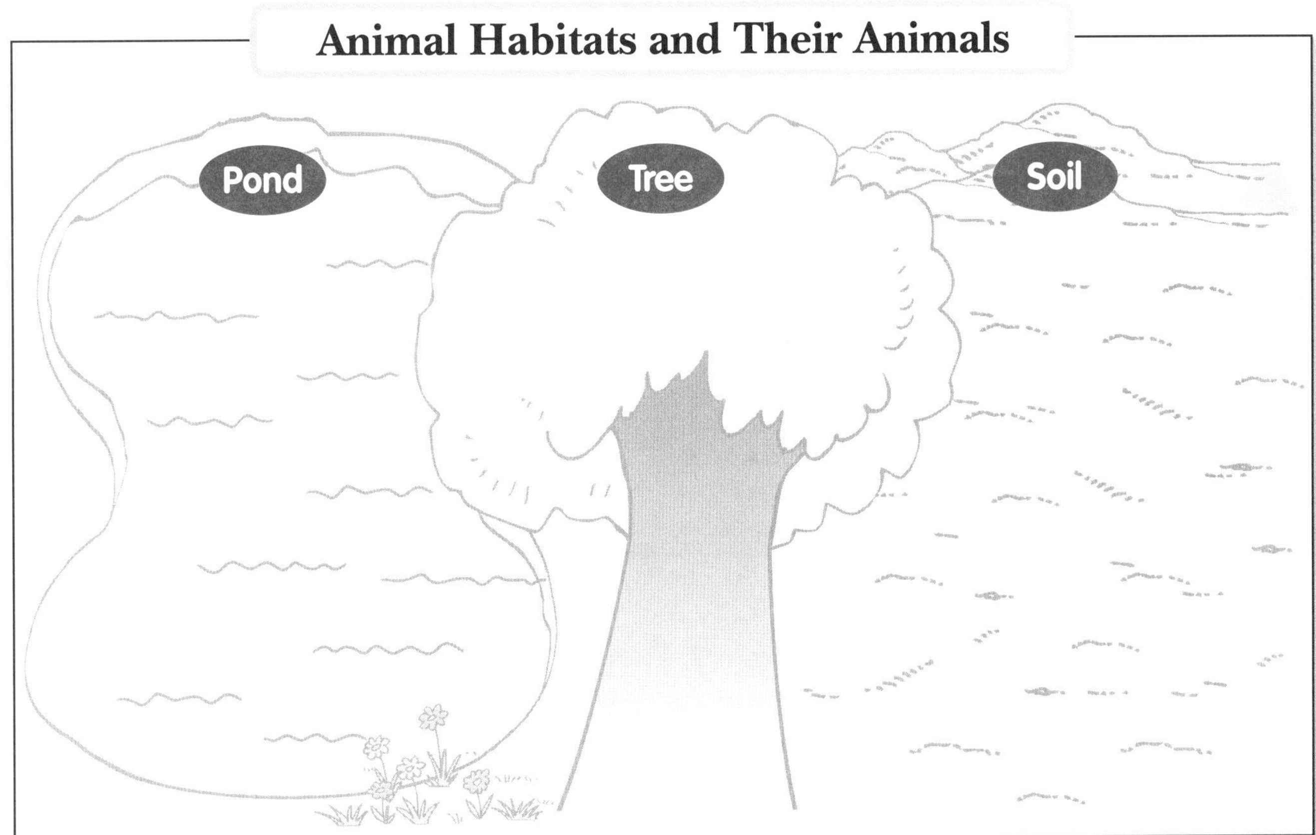

Week 2

SOCIAL STUDIES

A. There are many natural resources in the Appalachian Region. Find the natural products in the word search.

Natural Resources Word Search

potatoes blueberries oysters iron fish salt

oil lobsters Irish moss lumber hydro-electricity

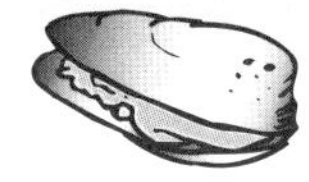

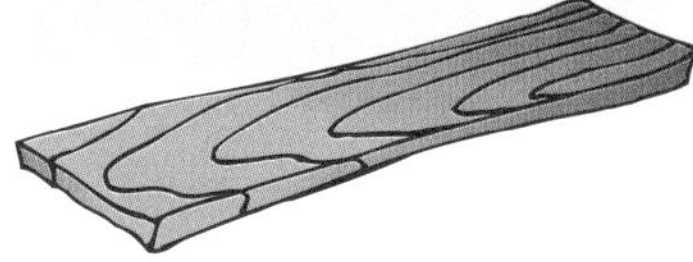

b	l	e	I	b	s	t	b	h		r	i	o	y	s	e	r
h	y	d	r	o	-	e	l	e	c	t	r	i	c	i	t	y
p	o	t	s	y	p	r	u	h	l	t	n	l	a	o	n	a
r	a	n	h	s	o	z	d	I	c	i	t	y	l	y	h	g
a	j	s	a	t	e	m	o	r	x	b	s	a	l	t	b	e
l	u	m	b	e	r	t	-	i	p	l	a	m	u	o	p	a
t	r	d		r	q	b	e		l	s	l	t	m	e	o	t
i	b	f	i	s	h	s	l	m	o	d	o	-	e	l	t	r
h	g	i	e	a	u	a	l	o	b	e	i	v	a	q	a	j
y	I	r	i	s	h		m	o	s	s	f	b	c	o	t	b
d	t	o	g	m	j	d	p	a	t	a	t	e	s	f	o	i
e	t	n	f	l	o	b	l	u	e	b	e	r	r	i	e	s
b	e	r	r	u	s	a	m	I	r	p	l	i		m	s	h
g	r	n	r	o	-	l	o	e	s	h	e	o	i	y	c	d
i	s	e	s	b	f	s	q	l	a	e	c	i	t	t	l	s

Can you guess what the most valuable resource is in the Atlantic provinces?

It's ________________ .

B. Every river system has six features. Read the clues and unscramble the words to find the features.

1. ________________ (c e r o s u) – where a river begins
2. ________________ (l o w f) – the movement of the river
3. ________________ (t a t r u r i b y) – smaller river or stream that flows into a larger river
4. ________________ (t o m h u) – where a river flows into another body of water
5. ________________ (c h a b r n) – a division of a river that has splits
6. ________________ (t a e l d) – area at mouth where rocks and earth have been deposited

Canada's capital city, Ottawa, is located where three rivers come together – the Gatineau, the Ottawa, and the Rideau.

C. Look at the map and fill in the blanks with the words in (B).

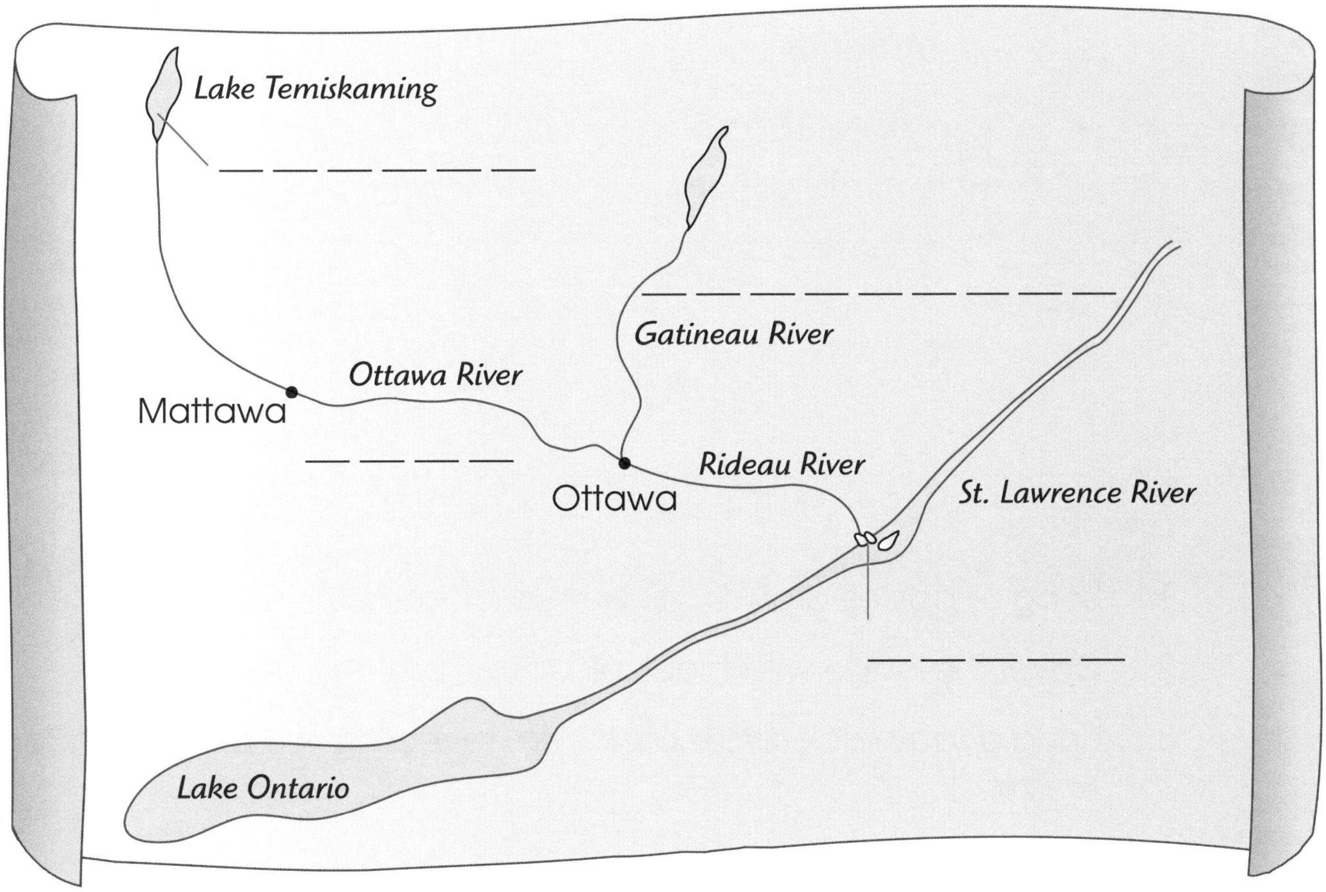

Neon

Materials:

- oil pastel
- white paper
- toothpick

Directions:

1. Using oil pastel, draw a rainbow of colours, filling the page.
2. Cover the page with black oil pastel, pressing heavily.
3. Using a toothpick, draw a picture, revealing the colours under the black.

Etching

A. The children are measuring their heights and weights. Help them record or show their measurements.

1. 

Jane

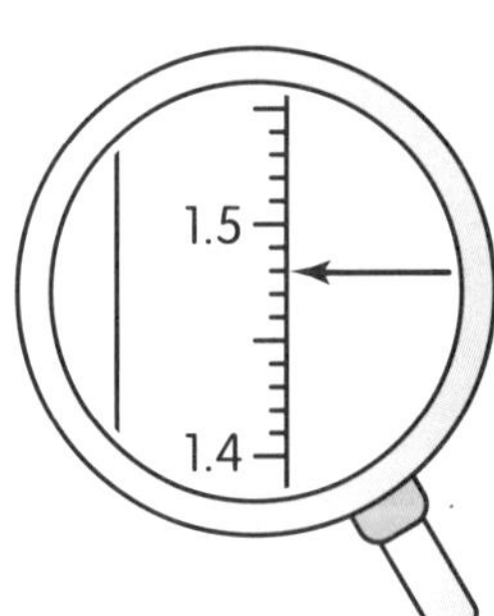

Weight : ________ kg

Height : ________ m

2. 

Andy

1.6
1.5

Weight : ________ kg

Height : ________ m

3. 

Ryan

36
37

1.4
1.3

Weight : ________ kg

Height : ________ m

4. 

Ruby

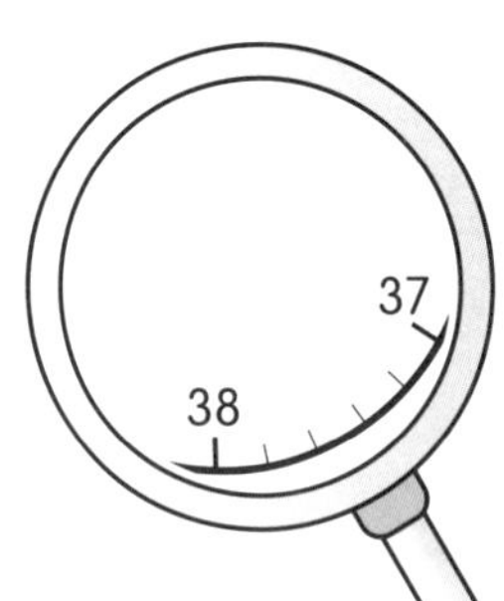

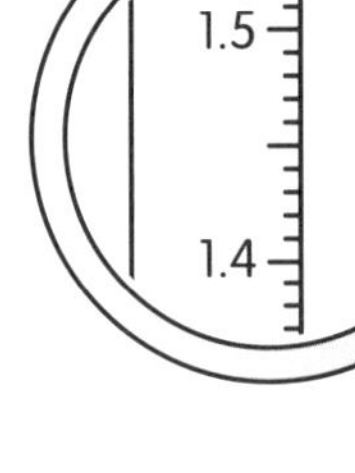

1.5
1.4

Weight : 37.7 kg

Height : 1.41 m

5. 

Sue

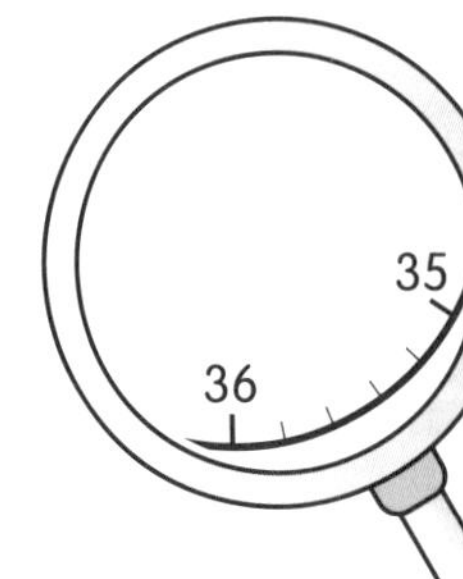

Weight : 35.6 kg

Height : 1.45 m

B. Look at the records in (A) again. Write the measurements in the lists. Then solve the problems.

3. 

I weighed 36.87 kg last year. How much have I gained?

______________________ = ________

Jane has gained ________ kg.

4. 

I was 1.49 m tall last year. How much have I grown?

______________________ = ________

Andy has grown ________ m.

5. 

My brother is 0.28 m taller than I. How tall is my brother?

______________________ = ________

Ryan's brother is ________ m tall.

C. **Mrs. Taylor records the heights of a group of students. Help her complete the graph. Then answer the questions.**

	Number of Children
Group A (110 cm to 119 cm)	卌 卌 ||
Group B (120 cm to 129 cm)	卌 卌 卌 |||
Group C (130 cm to 139 cm)	卌 卌 卌 卌 ||||
Group D (140 cm to 149 cm)	卌 卌 卌 |||
Group E (150 cm to 159 cm)	卌 |||

1.

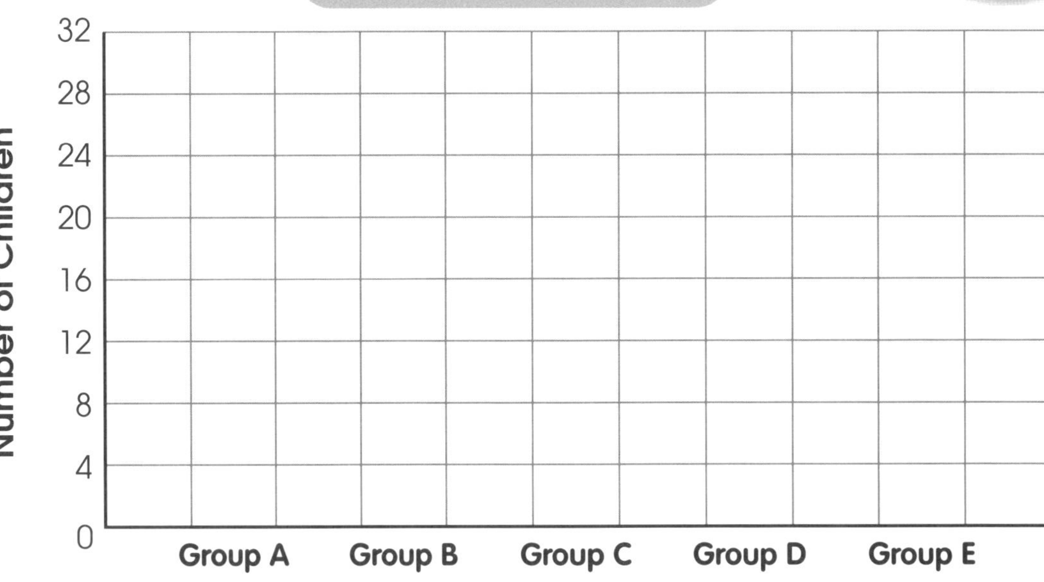

2. What is the range of the height of children in Group A? ____________

3. How many children have heights between 120 cm and 129 cm? ____________

4. Jonathan is 116 cm tall. In which group will Mrs. Taylor put Jonathan? Group ______

D. Mrs. Taylor is measuring things with the children. Help them complete the number sentences. Then solve the problems.

1. Jack weighs 38.5 kg. If Jack and a bag of sand weigh 47.4 kg, how heavy is a bag of sand?

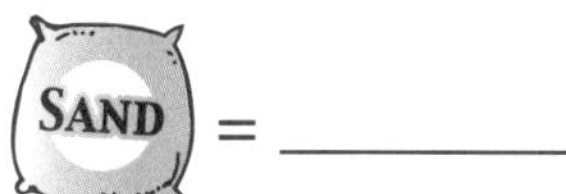

A bag of sand weighs ________ kg.

2. Gordon is 1.38 m tall. He is standing on a stool. If the height of Gordon with the stool is 1.54 m, what is the height of the stool?

The height of the stool is ________ m.

Help Aaron solve the problem.

A poster costs $4 at Ray-Mart. If Aaron joins their Collectors Club, the cost of the first poster will be $6.99 and each poster after that will cost $3. Which way should Aaron take to buy 5 posters? How much does he need to pay?

____

____

Hi, my name is Elizabeth and I would like to share with you a sport that I really enjoy. I hope that once you read about my favourite sport, you may be interested in giving it a try. My favourite sport is dog sledding. If you enjoy nature, like speed, and love dogs, then this is the sport for you!

Dog Sledding

I first became interested when I went on the trip of a lifetime to Alaska to see the world famous Iditarod Trail race. It is a dog sledding race that spans over the rough Alaskan terrain. While I was there, I had a chance to talk to some of the people involved in the sport and I found out that I could do this in my hometown of Sudbury, Ontario.

When I returned, my parents saw how excited I was and they bought me my first dog which I named Gunther. Soon after Gunther came Rocky, Chinook, and Harley. I began training my team when they were puppies. I started by working on basic commands. Then, we began endurance training by going on long jogs together. Next, I introduced them to wearing a harness and began teaching them dog sledding commands. Did you know that to start a team you say "hike", to turn right you say "gee", to turn left you say "haw", and to pass by something you say "on by"? I bet you can figure out what they do when I say "whoa"!

The best part about the training is that you can do it throughout the year. As my team grew bigger, I hooked them up to a gangline and had them tow me on a mountain bike and later they pulled me in a cart with wheels. When winter came, I had them tow me on skis and then finally the sled. The most important things to remember are to never, ever let go of the sled and always use the proper commands.

For now I am happy to enjoy the company of my team. Maybe one day I can enter the Iditarod and, who knows, maybe I'll even see you there!

A. Answer the following questions.

1. Why do you think Elizabeth enjoys dog sledding?

____

2. How did Elizabeth first get interested in her favourite sport?

____

3. Who are on Elizabeth's team?

____

4. What kind of training did Elizabeth do with the dogs in the summertime?

____

5. Name two things that dogs learn during their training.

____

6. Explain these terms as used in dog sledding:

   a. on by _______________

   b. haw _______________

   c. hike _______________

   d. gee _______________

B. Complete the following sentences with words from the passage.

1. Dog sledding is Elizabeth's _______________ sport.
2. The Iditarod Trail race _______________ over the rough Alaskan terrain.
3. Elizabeth has to train her dogs _______________ the year.
4. Giving _______________ commands is important in dog sledding.
5. Going on long jogs is part of the _______________ training.

C. **Elizabeth is telling you the sport of dog sledding. Choose a sport or an activity that interests you. Complete the planning sheet below so that you can share the information with your friends.**

Name of Sport

____

Type of Personality that this Sport Attracts

____

Equipment Required to Participate

____

Training Required

____

Rules of the Sport

____

A Brief Description of How It Is Played

____

____

Homophones *are words that sound alike but are spelled differently and have different meanings.*

D. Write the correct homophone in the correct blank.

week / weak	1. I was feeling ill and very ________ for about a ________ .
peek / peak	2. The dogs climbed to the ________ of the mountain. Elizabeth took a ________ over the edge.
to / too / two	3. My ________ dogs are ________ tired to continue the race. They will need ________ rest.
chilly / chilli	4. A great meal on a ________ night is a hot bowl of ________ .
scene / seen	5. The criminal was ________ at the ________ of the crime.
herd / heard	6. I ________ a ________ of cattle rushing towards us.

Challenge

Write a funny sentence using a pair of homophones.

____

____

LIGHT

A. Light enables us to see things. Test your knowledge about light by taking this "light" quiz. Circle the correct answers.

1. Light is _____ .

   A. a form of energy
   B. a type of gas
   C. a type of colour

2. An opaque object _____ .

   A. blocks light
   B. allows light to pass through it
   C. is opal coloured

3. Light travels _____ .

   A. in a bus from town to town
   B. in straight lines from the light source
   C. up and down the stairs, over and over again

4. When white light passes through a prism, it _____ .

   A. refracts, displaying the seven colours of the visible spectrum
   B. reflects, displaying the seven colours of the visible spectrum
   C. is absorbed

5. A pencil, when placed in a glass of water, appears to be broken because of _____ .

   A. reflection
   B. refraction
   C. absorption

6. A rainbow appears when ______ .
   A. the moon bends sunlight
   B. water drops in the air bend sunlight
   C. pots of gold are nearby

B. Here is a set of words that all have something to do with light. Use the related words after each blank to come up with the "light term".

1. ________________ (luminous, wax)
2. ________________ (luminous, night, insect)
3. ________________ (toy, colours, mirrors)
4. ________________ (glass, triangle, rectangle)
5. ________________ (lens, retina, cornea)
6. ________________ (storm, thunder, flashes)
7. ________________ (window pane glass, let light through)
8. ________________ (blocked light, opaque)

shadow
eyeball
lightning
candle
kaleidoscope
firefly
transparent
prism

Science Fun

The moon does not produce light on its own. We see it because sunlight bounces off it. It reflects sunlight.

A. Fill in the blanks to complete the definitions of the resources found in the Canadian Shield.

nickel gold fossil fuels silver
rivers forests lead copper

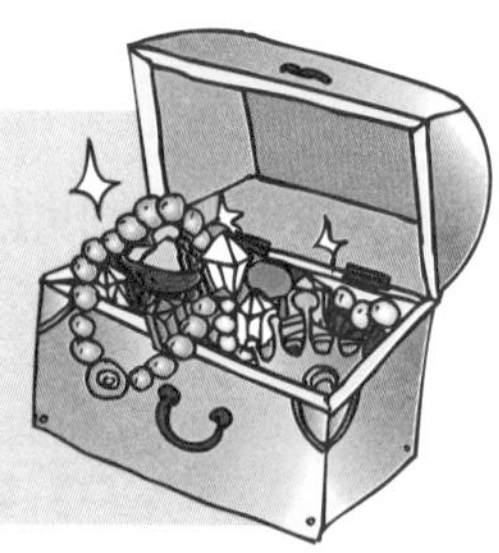

More than half of Canada is in the Canadian Shield. This area is well-known for its natural resources.

1. ______________ is a heavy, yellow precious metal, often used in making jewellery.
2. ______________ is a reddish-brown metal used as a conductor of electricity and heat.
3. ______________ is a whitish metal used in making coins. It has the same name as a Canadian coin with a beaver on it.
4. ______________ is a bluish-grey metal used in making pipes.
5. ______________ are thick growths of trees and underbrush.
6. ______________ is a white metal used in making mirrors and jewellery. It is also used in photography.

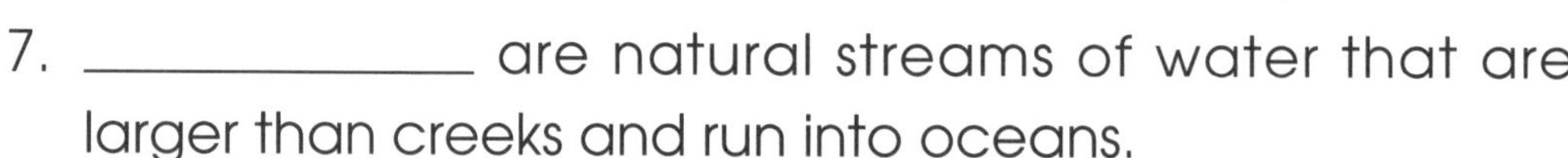

7. ______________ are natural streams of water that are larger than creeks and run into oceans.
8. ______________ are found mostly in the territories. They come from decayed animal bodies.

B. Read the clues and complete the crossword puzzle about things related to the Interior Plains.

Across

A. formed during the last ice age and found in the north of the Interior Plains

B. tiny pieces of rock, carried by rivers into the sea

C. This province lies between Saskatchewan and Ontario.

D. This type of mine is found in Saskatchewan.

Down

1. This province produces the most oil in Canada.

2. The most valuable natural resources in the Interior Plains are ___ fuels.

3. animals that roamed the Interior Plains millions of years ago

4. The Interior Plains stretch from the Arctic all the way to this country.

Did you know? Saskatchewan is the "breadbasket" of Canada because it produces over 54% of the wheat grown in Canada.

Materials:

- 1 empty dishwashing liquid bottle
- sandpaper
- newspaper strips
- wallpaper paste and water
- white paint
- fabric scrap
- black cardboard
- glue
- brush
- googly eyes
- yarn

Snow Sculpture

Directions:

1. Sand bottle to make surface rough.
2. Dip newspaper into wallpaper paste and cover bottle.
3. Repeat (2) and let dry.
4. Paint sculpture white.
5. Glue googly eyes and yarn for mouth.
6. Make a hat, using black cardboard. Glue to “head”.
7. Make a small scarf from fabric scrap and wrap around “neck” of sculpture.

Week 4

MATHEMATICS

A. **Read what Jason says. Write the names of the shapes on the lines. Then draw the shapes in the boxes.**

Please help me sort the shapes.

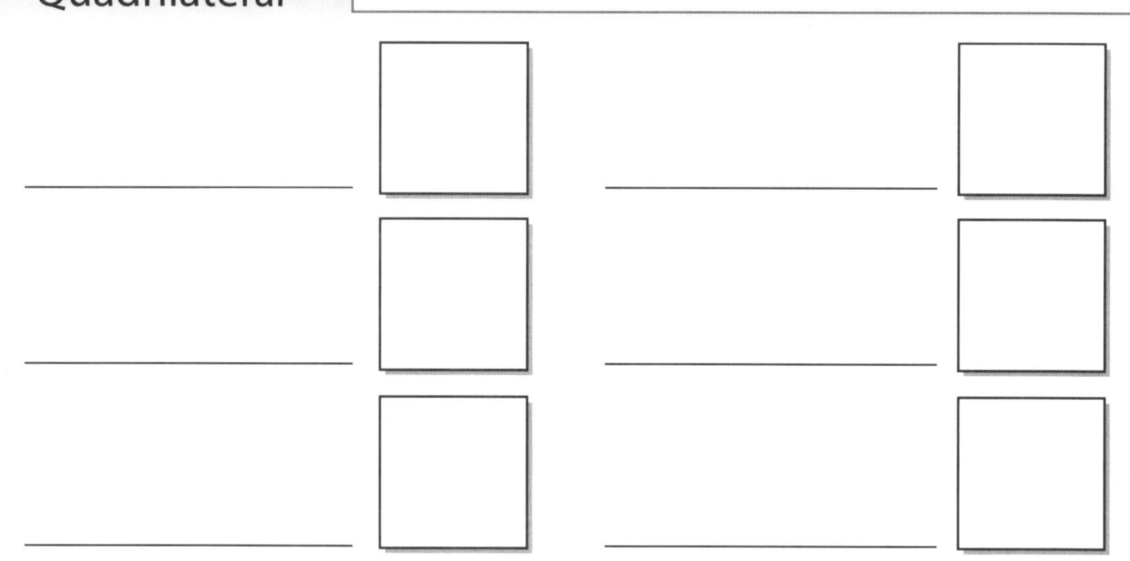

Circle
Trapezoid
Square
Rectangle
Parallelogram
Kite
Pentagon
Triangle
Rhombus
Hexagon

Quadrilateral

Not Quadrilateral

B. Look at the children's pictures and read what the children say. Check ✔ the correct letters to answer their questions.

1. *Which one shows the rotation image of my picture?*

2. *Which one shows the reflection image of my picture?*

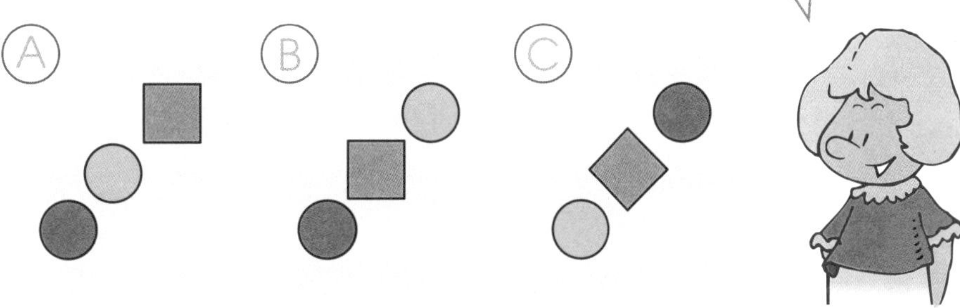

3. 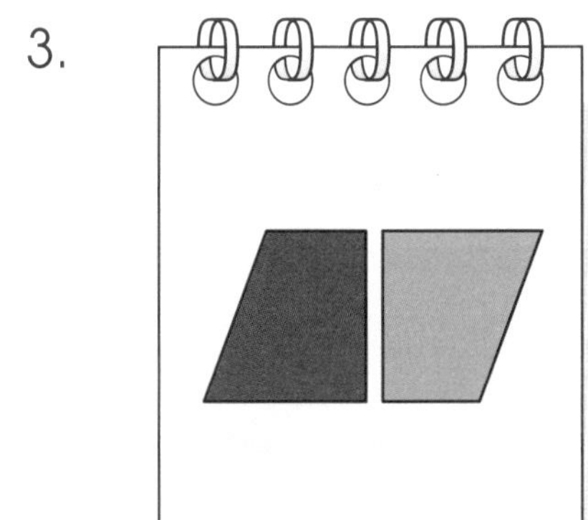

Which one shows the translation image of my picture?

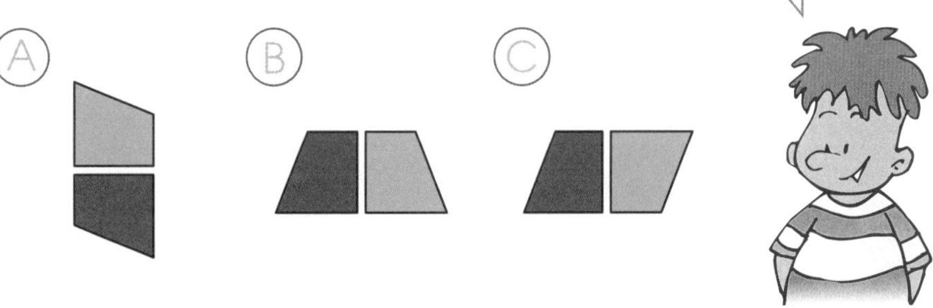

4. 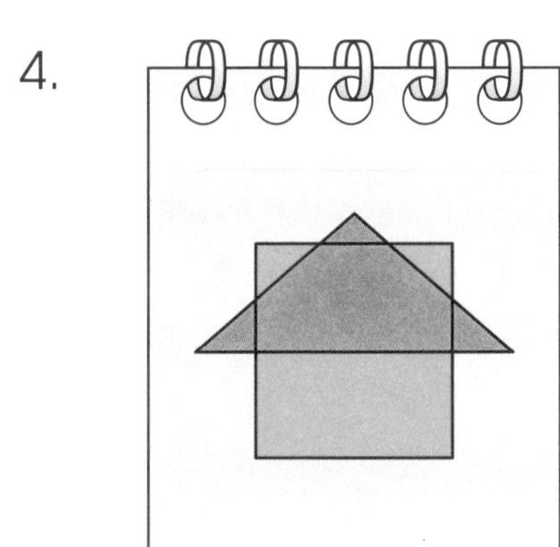

Which one is not the rotation image of my picture?

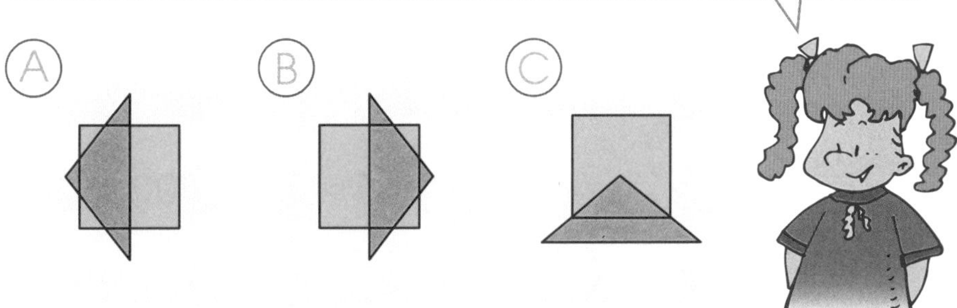

C. **Jason drew 2 groups of shapes. Find what things are common in each group. Help Jason check ✓ the correct sentences. Put a cross ✗ for the wrong ones.**

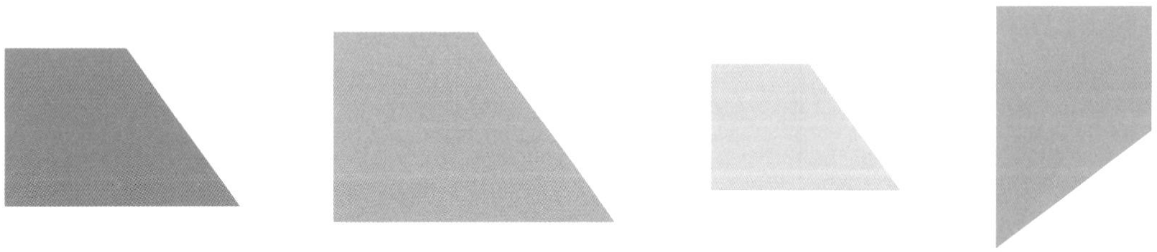

1. They are congruent. ◯
2. They are trapezoids. ◯
3. Each shape has 2 right angles. ◯
4. Each shape has 4 equal sides. ◯
5. Each shape can be formed by 2 triangles. ◯
6. Each shape has 1 line of symmetry. ◯

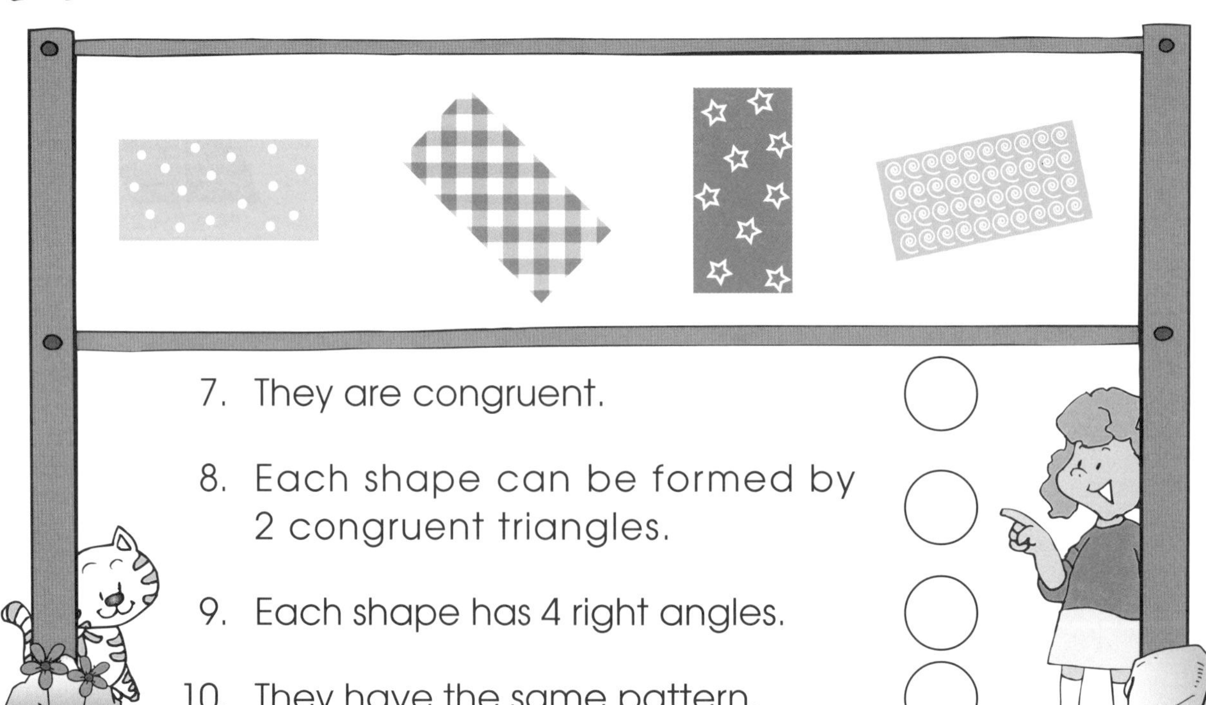

7. They are congruent. ◯
8. Each shape can be formed by 2 congruent triangles. ◯
9. Each shape has 4 right angles. ◯
10. They have the same pattern. ◯

D. Each child drew half of a shape. Measure each side of the incomplete shape and draw the other half. Then find how many lines of symmetry each shape has.

1. ______ line(s) of symmetry	2. ______ line(s) of symmetry
3. 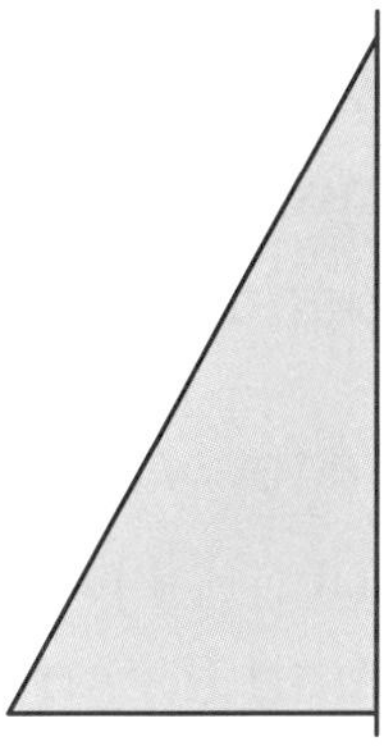 ______ line(s) of symmetry	4. 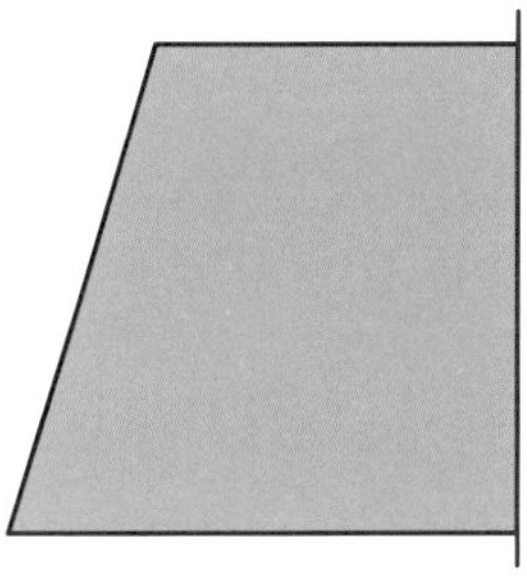 ______ line(s) of symmetry

Find the masses of the toys.

If the car and the soldier have the same mass and the mass of the piggy bank is 2 times that of the soldier, what is the mass of each toy?

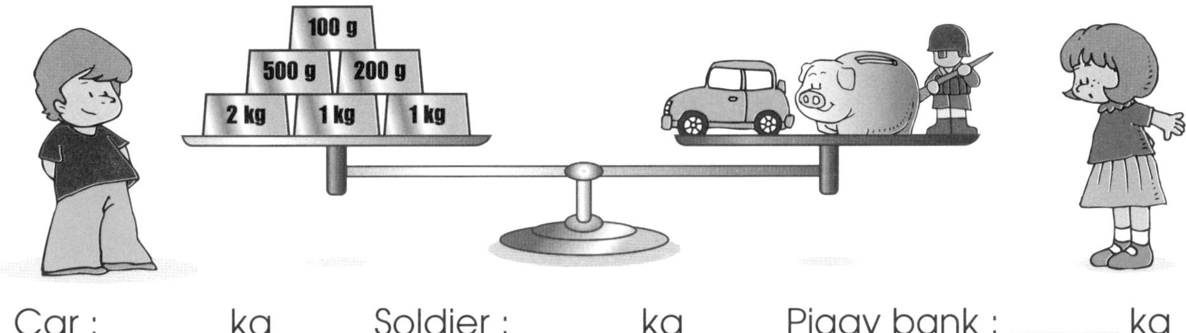

Car : ______ kg Soldier : ______ kg Piggy bank : ______ kg

No Problem

The other day, I learned that operating the dishwasher is not as easy as it seems. It was a bright, sunny, summer day. I had just come in from mowing the lawn when the phone rang. It was my mom. She told me to start the dishwasher once I had finished my lunch. "No problem," I said as I secretly rolled my eyes. My mom usually called every day with some new job to keep me busy. I figured I had got off easily this time because all I had to do was put the soap in and turn the dishwasher on.

When I poured the powdered soap into the slot, a few crystals trickled out of the box. It was empty. "No problem," I thought. "I'll just get some more." I looked in every cupboard and could not find any more. "No problem," I thought. "I can use the liquid soap by the sink." I filled the slot with the gooey, yellow solution, closed the door, and pushed "Start". With a spring in my step, I headed next door to see if Kyle would like to play some video games.

About 10 minutes later, Kyle and I came back to my house all ready for an afternoon of fun. I was shocked when I entered the kitchen and found myself waist-high in soapsuds. As Kyle went on about how cool it looked, I decided to grab a bucket and start scooping. "No problem," I thought. "We can get this cleaned up in no time."

An hour later, I was still waist high in suds and the backyard was beginning to look like a freaky winter scene. When I turned to talk to Kyle, he had disappeared. I thought he sensed that my mom would soon be home.

Just as I thought of her, there she was. I had to think quickly. "No problem," I thought. "I'll just shrink down into these suds and she'll never find me." I was wrong!

A. Write "T" for the true sentences and "F" for the false ones.

1. ______ This story took place during summer holidays.
2. ______ This was the first time the mother had called asking for a job to be done.
3. ______ There were not enough soap crystals to start the machine.
4. ______ The boy in the story thought of himself as a good problem-solver.
5. ______ Liquid soap is a good substitute when you don't have powdered soap to put in your dishwasher.
6. ______ The liquid soap created lots of suds.
7. ______ The disaster was easily cleaned before the mother returned home.
8. ______ Hiding in the soapsuds was a good idea.

B. Find from the passage words that rhyme with the following.

1. buds ______________
2. knowing ______________
3. prawn ______________
4. wink ______________
5. spot ______________
6. tab ______________
7. knight ______________
8. petals ______________
9. soared ______________
10. bound ______________
11. cope ______________
12. cling ______________

Rhyming Words

A **limerick** is a funny poem.

There once was a boy named Rob
Whose mother had given him a job.
The soapbox was empty,
Ideas he had plenty,
In deep suds his name became Bob.

C. Write your own limerick using the following information.

- A limerick has five lines.
- Lines one, two, and five rhyme and they have the same length and rhythm.
- Lines three and four rhyme. They are shorter than the other lines.
- Most limericks begin with **There once was a...**

Line 1: ____________________

Line 2: ____________________

Line 3: ____________________

Line 4: ____________________

Line 5: ____________________

D. Circle the adjective or adjectives that describe each underlined noun in the sentences below.

1. It was a bright, sunny <u>day</u>.
2. I poured the powdered <u>soap</u> into the dishwasher.
3. I filled the slot with the gooey, yellow <u>solution</u>.
4. The bubbly <u>suds</u> filled the kitchen.
5. The quiet and peaceful <u>day</u> turned into a nightmare.

E. Use each pair of adjectives listed below in a sentence.

1. big and fluffy

   ____

2. soft and smooth

   ____

3. smart and confident

   ____

4. tiny and delicate

   ____

F. Draw a cartoon strip that shows the events in this story. Use talk balloons to show what the characters are saying or thinking.

A. **There are three types of rocks. Read about them and complete the statements.**

ROCKS

volcano igneous granite metamorphic marble sedimentary pressure limestone

Week 4

SCIENCE

1. Melted rock deep in the Earth comes up through the crust, sometimes as molten lava through a ________________ . It cools and hardens. This is ________________ rock. Basalt, ________________ , and pumice are examples of this kind of rock.

2. The Earth changes and some rocks get buried. Heat or ________________ changes them, without melting them. Now they are ________________ rocks. Gneiss, slate, and ________________ are examples of this kind of rock.

3. The wind, rain, and gravity broke down pieces of bigger rock and sand. They collected and settled, layer upon layer. Millions of years later, they are ________________ rocks. Examples of this kind of rock are sandstone, ________________ , and shale.

Science Fun

Some rocks fall from the sky! Very rare, meteorites are rocks that have entered Earth's atmosphere from space.

B. Try this!

Is there air in rocks?

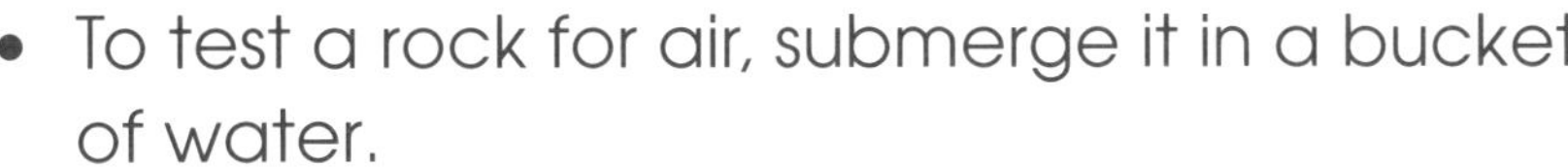

- To test a rock for air, submerge it in a bucket of water.

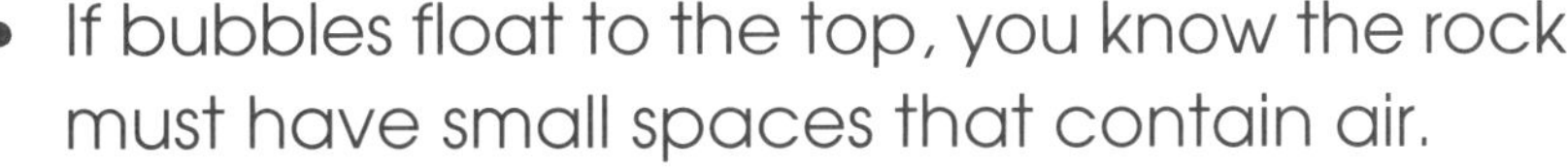

- If bubbles float to the top, you know the rock must have small spaces that contain air.

C. Write the letters of the things that are made from rock in the box.

A B C D E F

Become a Rockhound

Rocks are the oldest things you can collect, and they're everywhere.

Record their size, colour, shape, texture, and lustre.

*The **Feudal System** was a way of sharing land in the time around 1200 C.E. It worked like a pyramid, with the king at the top and the peasants at the bottom.*

A. Read the descriptions below and write the numbers in the correct parts of the pyramid.

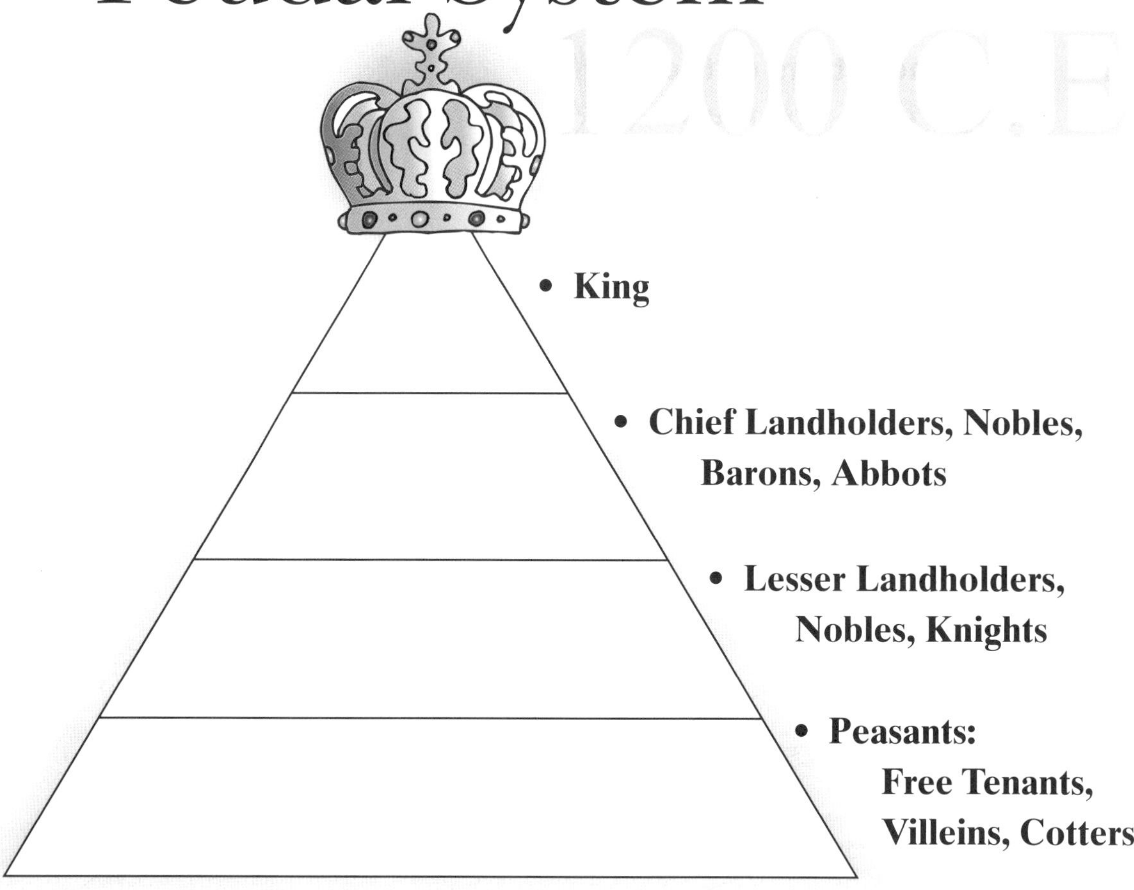

1. Divided up land among followers they wanted to reward.
2. Owned all the land.
3. Promised to be faithful to the chief landholder.
4. Kept a portion of all land for his own use.
5. Divided up some of their land among peasants.
6. Promised to obey the lesser landholder and tend to the land.
7. Divided up the rest of the land among his most important men.
8. Had no land of their own.

B. Read about a manor and answer the questions that follow.

The feudal estate was the manor, which consisted of a manor house, one or more villages, and lots of land. The lord of the manor was often a knight. He often had more than one manor. He spent much of his time visiting his manors and hunting. While he was away, the lady of the manor was in charge.

There were many people who ran the lord's manors. The steward was in charge of all of them. He visited all the manors governed by his lord. The day-to-day manager of each estate and chief law officer was the bailiff. The reeve was one of the peasants who supervised the villagers in each manor.

The peasants were divided into three groups: the free tenants, who paid rent for their land, the villeins, who paid for their land in services, and the cotters, who had little or no land at all.

1. Who was usually the lord of the manor?

   ____

2. Who were the people that ran the manor?

   ____

3. Describe the people named.

   a. free tenants: ______________________________

   b. cotters: ______________________________

   c. villeins: ______________________________

Pebble Poem

Materials:

- foil
- styrofoam tray
- hot glue gun
- fabric or ribbon strips
- several small, smooth pebbles
- black permanent marker

Directions:

1. Wash pebbles in water.
2. Let dry on paper towels.
3. Compose simple poem or saying like "I love you rocks".
4. Using black permanent marker, write one letter on each pebble.
5. Cover both sides of styrofoam tray with foil.
6. On inside, arrange poem or saying in a creative way.
7. Use hot glue to "set" each pebble.
8. Use ribbon or fabric strips to make a frame, hot gluing in place.

A. It is 2007. Dr. Pronk has just invented a time machine. The machine can take him to different times in the past. Help Dr. Pronk find the years of invention.

1.

Airplane

Time from invention to present :
1 century and 4 years

Year of invention : ________

2.

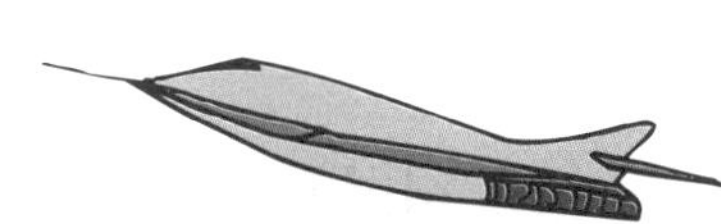

Supersonic jet

Time from invention to present :
5 decades and 4 years

Year of invention : ________

3.

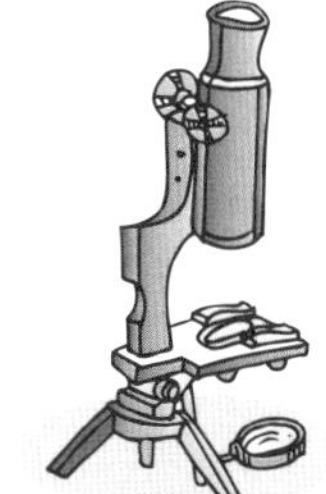

Electron microscope

Time from invention to present :
7 decades and 4 years

Year of invention : ________

4.

Hot air balloon

Time from invention to present :
2 centuries and 24 years

Year of invention : ________

5.

Watch

Time from invention to present :
Half a millennium and 45 years

Year of invention : ________

B. The time machine has taken Dr. Pronk to the future. Look at the things that Dr. Pronk sees during his travel. Write the number of faces that each thing has and complete the sentences.

1. 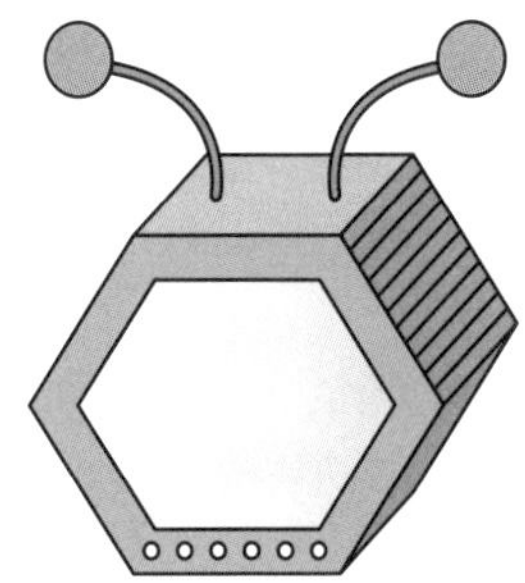

3D TV

It has ______ faces.

It has ______ rectangular face(s), ______ hexagonal face(s), and ______ triangular face(s).

2. 

Smart Tool

It has ______ faces.

It has ______ rectangular face(s), ______ square face(s), and ______ triangular face(s).

3. 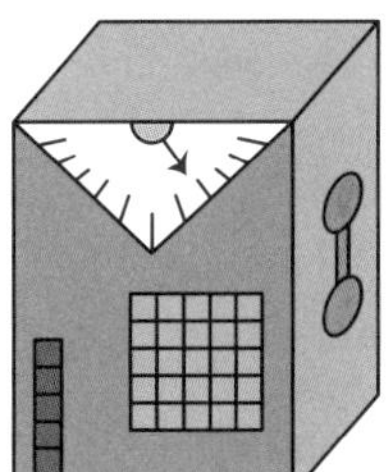

Secret Cook

It has ______ faces.

It has ______ rectangular face(s), ______ square face(s), and ______ triangular face(s).

4. 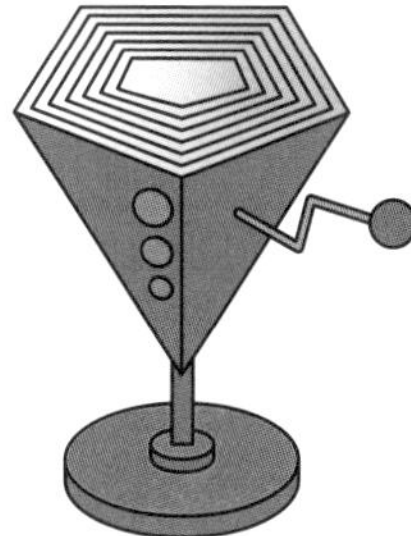

Super Alarm

It has ______ faces.

It has ______ rectangular face(s), ______ pentagonal face(s), and ______ triangular face(s).

5. 

Foldable Robot

It has ______ faces.

It has ______ rectangular face(s), ______ square face(s), and ______ triangular face(s).

C. **Dr. Pronk drove his time machine to different places in different years. Help him find the travelling times and the times spent in the given years.**

Arrival time : 10:59 a.m.
Departure time : 12:45 a.m.

Arrival time : 2:27 p.m.
Departure time : 4:45 p.m.

Departure time : 10:45 a.m.

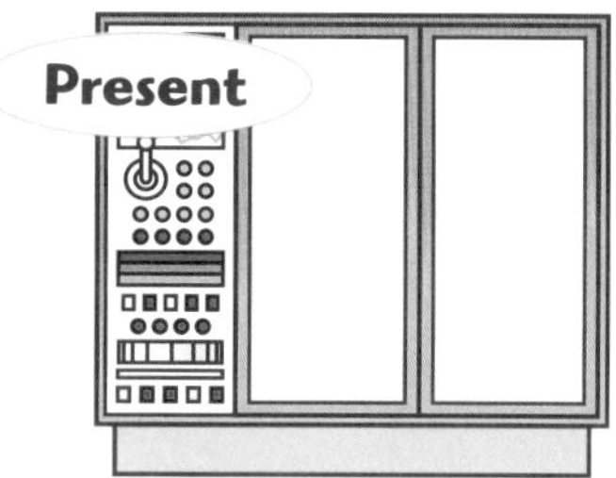

Arrival time : 4:57 a.m.
Departure time : 6:16 a.m.

Arrival time : 8:45 p.m.

1. **Travelling time**

From the present to 1935: ______ minutes

From 1935 to 1985 : ______ minutes

From 2015 to the present: ______ minutes

2. **Time spent**

In 1935 : ______ hour and ______ minutes ; ______ minutes in all

In 1985 : ______ hour and ______ minutes ; ______ minutes in all

In 2015 : ______ hour and ______ minutes ; ______ minutes in all

Week 5

MATHEMATICS

D. Dr. Pronk comes across some robots. Colour the keypads and help him activate the robots.

1.

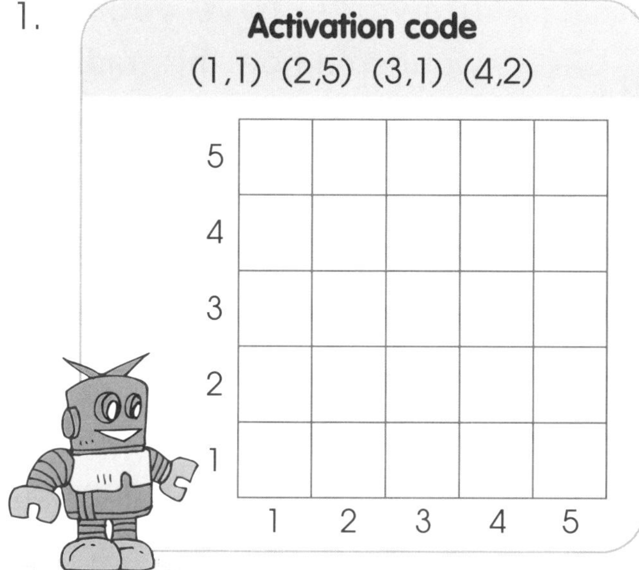

2.

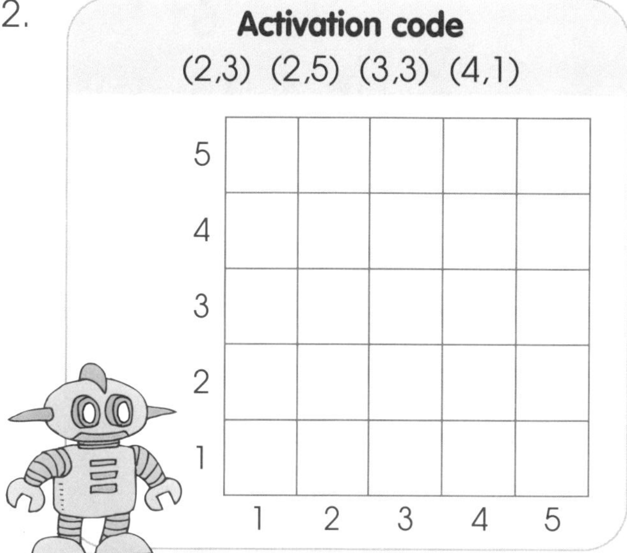

3.

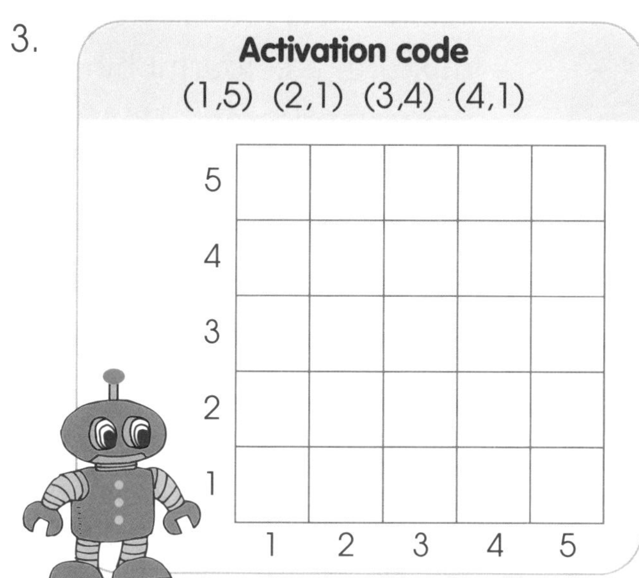

4.

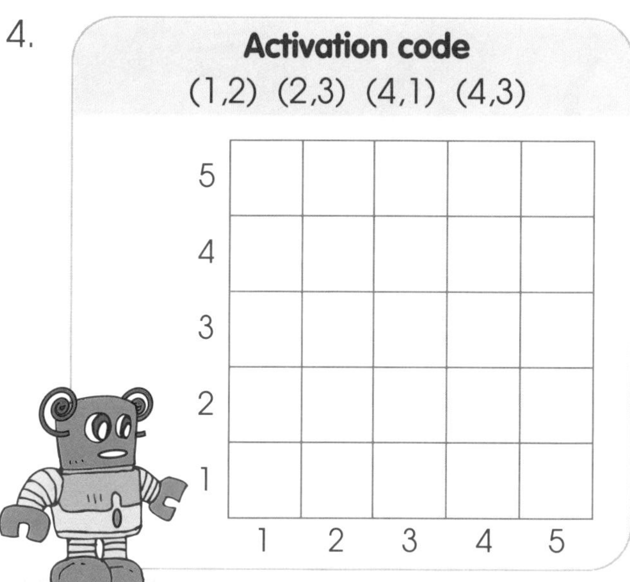

Help Bob the Robot Astronaut solve the problem.

I drank 12 L of gas on Wednesday. I drank 10 times more on Thursday and 100 times more on Friday. How many litres of gas did I drink in the past three days?

Bob drank ______ litres of gas in all.

The History of Fireworks

When witnessing a spectacular display of fireworks, have you ever wondered how this tradition first got its start? You would be surprised to learn that this discovery happened over one thousand years ago in the kitchen of a Chinese chef. The chef accidentally mixed together the common ingredients of black powder, saltpetre, charcoal, and sulphur. As soon as he lit the mixture, a colourful burst of flames appeared. He began to experiment with this discovery. He noticed that if the mixture was put in the hollow of a bamboo shoot, a larger explosion occurred. The Chinese continued to experiment and eventually invented fireworks that could shoot into the air. They began to use fireworks to scare away enemies and evil spirits and to celebrate weddings, victories in battles, and religious ceremonies.

Over the next several hundred years, the knowledge of making fireworks spread west through Arabia to Italy and England. By 1600, firework displays made their way to North America. Fireworks became more spectacular in the 1800s. The Italians discovered that by adding potassium chlorate to the mixture, the fireworks would burn hotter and faster. This breakthrough led to the addition of colour, sparks, and flashes.

Today, computers are used to control firework displays that are timed to music. These extravaganzas still depend on the knowledge that has been passed on through many generations and civilizations. A firework expert combines traditional methods, simple materials, and a creative spirit to be both a scientist and an artist of pyrotechnology.

A. Put the events in order. Write 1 to 7.

______ Firework displays made their way to North America.

______ Computers are used to time firework displays with music.

______ The firework mixture was put into a bamboo shoot to create larger explosions.

______ The knowledge of firework making spread west.

______ A Chinese chef discovered the four ingredients which created a burst of flames.

______ The Italians discovered how to make fireworks burn hotter and faster.

______ Colour, sparks, and flashes were added to fireworks.

B. Complete the sentences with words from the passage.

1. It was a chef in China who ____________ invented fireworks.
2. The colourful ____________ of flames was the first firework display.
3. The chef began to ____________ with his discovery.
4. Fireworks were first used in battles to ____________ away enemies.
5. Fireworks were also used to ____________ weddings, victories in battles, and religious ceremonies.
6. The ____________ discovered how to add colour, sparks, and flashes to firework displays.
7. Computers enable firework displays to be ____________ to music.
8. Every summer, there is a ____________ display of fireworks at the Ontario Place.

C. **Adverbs and adverb phrases describe verbs. They tell where, when, or how something happens. Underline the adverbs and adverb phrases in the sentences.**

1. The fireworks exploded loudly.
2. The firework display ended quickly.
3. The chef worked in the kitchen.
4. The children walked to the park.

5. I exercise every Monday and Wednesday.

6. The old man moved very slowly.

7. The fireworks shone brightly in the night sky.
8. The guests will arrive soon.

D. **Adjectives tell more about nouns. Enrich the following sentences by adding adjectives. Write the new sentences on the lines.**

1. The boy drew a picture of firework displays.

   ____

2. There are shells on the beach.

   ____

3. I like swimming in the water on a summer day.

   ____

4. The children all want a popsicle.

   ____

5. We can see stars in the night sky.

   ____

E. Some words help you hear the sound when you say them. This is called Onomatopoeia. Use each of the following sound words in a complete sentence.

The bang of the fireworks woke up the neighbours.

1. buzz ______________________________
2. crash ______________________________
3. hiss ______________________________
4. sizzle ______________________________
5. roar ______________________________
6. splash ______________________________
7. pop ______________________________

F. Imagine that you were the Chinese chef. Write how you accidentally discovered fireworks.

WEATHER

When talking about weather, temperature is the degree of how hot or cold the environment is. We use the Celsius scale to compare this hotness or coldness.

A. Choose the reading that best describes the environment for each statement and write the letter in the box.

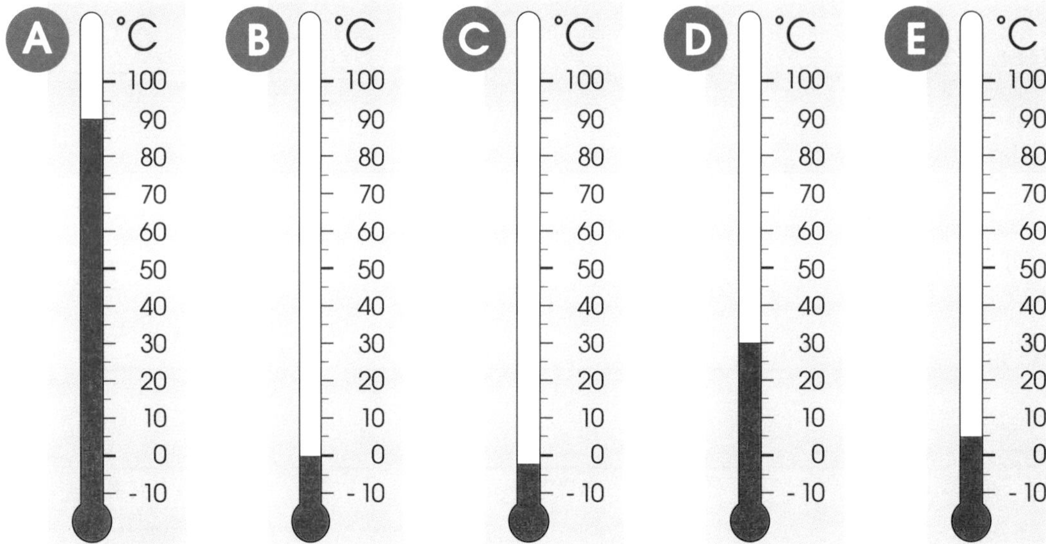

1.  *Brr! Winter must be here!* ☐

2. *Water freezes at this temperature.* ☐

3.  *Water in an ice cube tray is very cold but not quite frozen.* ☐

4.  *Water in a kettle is close to boiling.* ☐

5.  *Hot summer day. Lemonade anyone?* ☐

B. Where is all the water on Earth? Read the hints and write the letters in the boxes.

A. in all living things
B. in oceans
C. in rocks and soil
D. in glacial ice
E. in lakes or rivers

1. On highest mountains, and at north and south poles ☐
2. They cover about 70% of Earth's surface. ☐
3. Under your feet, could be hard or soft ☐
4. You, a chicken, a plant... ☐
5. They're moving fast, or maybe slow. ☐

C. Label what you see happening in this diagram of the water cycle.

A. Evaporation
B. Transpiration
C. Condensation
D. Precipitation
E. Collection

The Medieval Period of history began about 1500 years ago and ended about 500 years ago.

A. How did a peasant girl or a nobleman's daughter in the Medieval Period spend her day? Is it like your day or is it different? Read these statements and check ✔ "Same" or "Different".

		Same	Different
1.	I sleep on a straw pallet.	_____	_____
2.	I dress in my tunic.	_____	_____
3.	I can count up to 20.	_____	_____
4.	I can't read or write.	_____	_____
5.	I have bread and water for breakfast.	_____	_____
6.	I feed my geese every day.	_____	_____
7.	I work in the fields with the sheep.	_____	_____
8.	I snuggle in my comfortable bed.	_____	_____
9.	I eat meat for dinner.	_____	_____
10.	I wear nice clothes.	_____	_____

Is your day more like that of the peasant girl (1-7) or the nobleman's daughter (8-10)?

B. Fill in the missing words to complete the tale of a knight in the Medieval Period.

manor dubbed armour
sleeping servant prayed
lord eating dress lady
squire mother knight page

Hello! I am Sir Gal Ahad, of King Arthur's court. Let me tell you about how I came to be a 1.__________. I was born to a knight and his wife, my 2.__________. When I was about six years old, I became a 3.__________. I was trained by the 4.__________ of the castle. A page helps his lord 5.__________ and put on his 6.__________. My manners I learned from the ladies of the 7.__________. I waited on my lord and his 8.__________. At 14, I became a 9.__________. A squire is a knight's personal 10.__________.

The night before I became a knight, I 11.__________ without 12.__________ or 13.__________. The next day, my lord 14.__________ me "Sir Knight".

Frame for Mother's Day

Materials:

- heavy cardboard
- xacto knife
- sequins
- photo of you
- hot glue gun
- fabric (about 1/4 metre)
- pencil and ruler
- cotton balls
- cord

Directions:

1. Cut out front and back of frame (add 5 cm to each side of your photo).

2. Cut out centre of front piece (0.5 cm shorter for each side of photo).

3. Cover front piece with cotton balls.

4. Wrap front piece with fabric pieces. Hot glue.

5. Glue sequins on front piece to form beautiful pattern.

6. Make two holes on back piece and add cord to form hanger.

7. Place photo onto inside of back piece.

8. Cover with front piece. Glue into place.

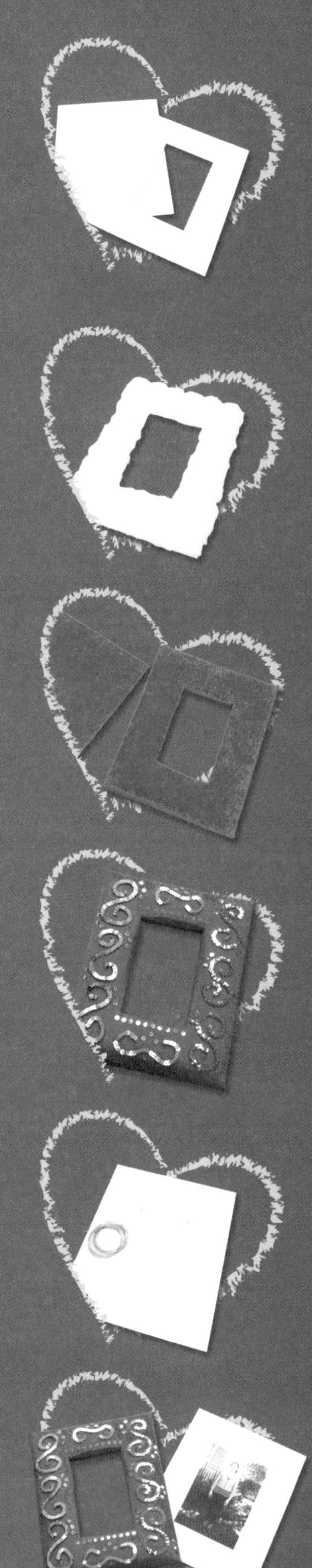

A. **Look at the toys the children are going to buy. Help them solve the problems.**

1. Louis buys a pack of cards and a toy car. How much does he need to pay?

____

2. Edward has $25. Does Edward have enough money to buy a box of puzzle and a yo-yo?

____

3. Ryan pays $40 for 2 boxes of cards and a toy car. What is his change?

____

4. The sale price of a box of puzzle is $12.99. Wilson wants to buy 2 boxes of puzzle. How much will he save?

____

B. Louis is playing cards with his friends. See what cards the children pick. Help them compare the outcomes with the given expressions.

More probable	Equally probable	Less probable

1. The chance of picking a  compared to a 

 ____

2. The chance of picking a  compared to a 

 ____

3. The chance of picking a  compared to a 

 ____

C. Circle the correct card to complete each sentence.

1. Each child has the greatest chance to pick a 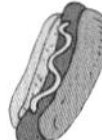  

.

2. Each child has the smallest chance to pick a 

  .

D. **Bruce picked a card and got a pizza. See how Bruce shares his pizza with his friends. Write a fraction and a decimal number in words to show how much pizza each child has.**

1. Bruce eats —— or ______ tenths of a pizza.

2. Ryan eats —— or ______________ of a pizza.

3. Wilson eats —— or ______________ of a pizza.

4. Edward eats —— or ______________ of a pizza.

E. **Answer the questions.**

1. Who has the most pizza? ______

2. Who has the least pizza? ______

3. Each slice of pizza weighs 198 g. How many grams of pizza

   a. does Bruce have? ______

   b. does Ryan have? ______

   c. does Wilson have? ______

   d. does Edward have? ______

4. Does the pizza weigh more than 2 kg? ______

Week 6

MATHEMATICS

F. The children each have their sets of cards. They pick a card each time without looking at it for 50 times. Predict the outcomes and check ✓ the correct letters.

1.

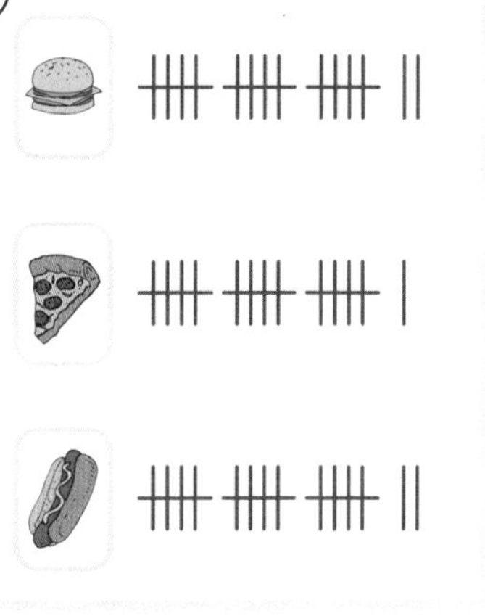

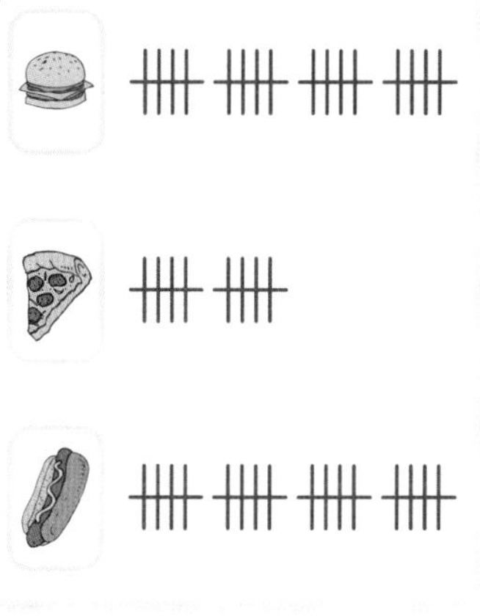

Card	Ⓐ	Ⓑ
hamburger	𝍸 𝍸 𝍸 ||	𝍸 𝍸 𝍸 𝍸
pizza	𝍸 𝍸 𝍸 |	𝍸 𝍸
hot dog	𝍸 𝍸 𝍸 ||	𝍸 𝍸 𝍸 𝍸

2.

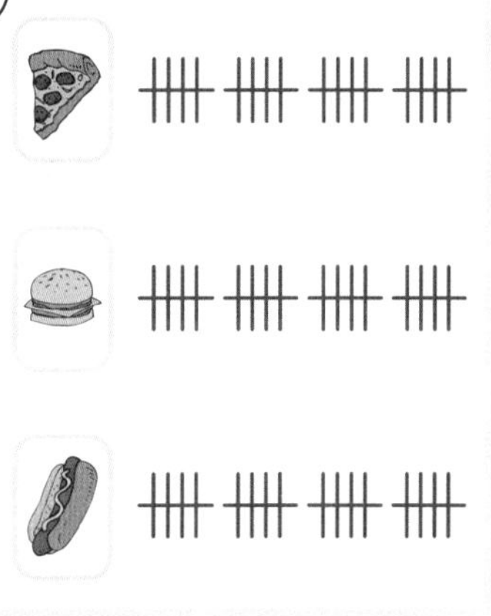

Card	Ⓐ	Ⓑ
pizza	𝍸 𝍸 𝍸 𝍸	𝍸 𝍸 𝍸 𝍸 𝍸 |||
hamburger	𝍸 𝍸 𝍸 𝍸	𝍸 𝍸
hot dog	𝍸 𝍸 𝍸 𝍸	𝍸 𝍸 ||

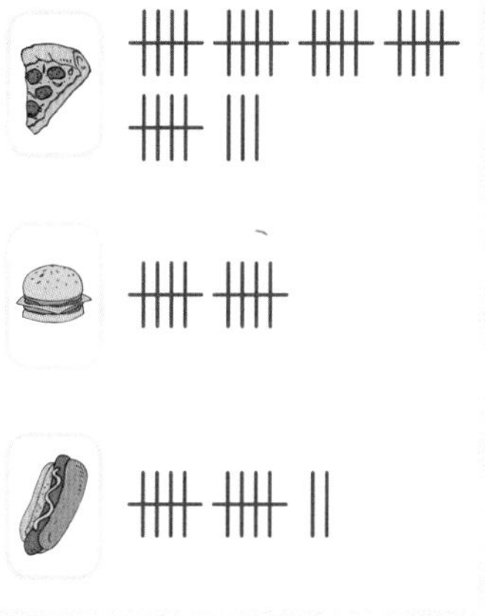

Read what John says. Answer his question.

The number of cards I have is less than 20. If I count by 2's or 3's, there will be 1 card left. If I count by 4's, there will be 3 cards left. If I count by 5's, there will be 4 cards left. How many cards do I have?

John has ________ cards.

Mia Hamm

Mia Hamm is widely known as the world's best female soccer player. She rose to fame as a member of the U.S. National Soccer Team at the age of 15, and at 19 she was the youngest member of the 1991 Women's World Cup Team.

Mia recruited her five brothers and sisters to be her soccer team when she was just seven years old. Mia was very competitive and loved to play games. She hated losing so much that if a game was not going her way, she would walk off the field. Her brothers and sisters refused to play with her unless she stuck with the game.

When she was in high school, a university scout recognized her talent and recruited her to the University of North Carolina. She assisted her team in winning four NCAA championships. She moved onto great successes as part of the U.S. National Soccer Team and was named U.S. Soccer's Female Athlete of the Year for five years in a row.

Besides being an outstanding athlete, Mia has worked hard to begin the Mia Hamm Foundation for Bone Marrow Research. Mia also spends time speaking to young women and encouraging them to develop their talents in sports. She is the author of an inspirational book called "Go for the Goal: A Champion's Guide to Winning in Soccer and Life". Mia truly gives one hundred percent both on and off the field.

A. Answer the following questions.

1. Why did Mia's brothers and sisters sometimes refuse to play soccer with Mia?

____

____

2. How did Mia join the University of North Carolina soccer team?

____

____

3. Explain in your own words "Mia truly gives one hundred percent both on and off the field."

____

____

____

B. Read the statements below. Decide whether each of them represents a fact (F) or an opinion (O).

1. _____ Mia is better than any male soccer player.
2. _____ Mia has five brothers and sisters.
3. _____ Mia has always loved the game of soccer.
4. _____ Mia should have focused on school rather than sports.
5. _____ Mia is a giving person.
6. _____ Mia speaks to young women and encourages them to develop their talents in sports.
7. _____ As a child, Mia should have been encouraged to pursue other interests.

C. **Choose the best heading for each of the following groups of words.**

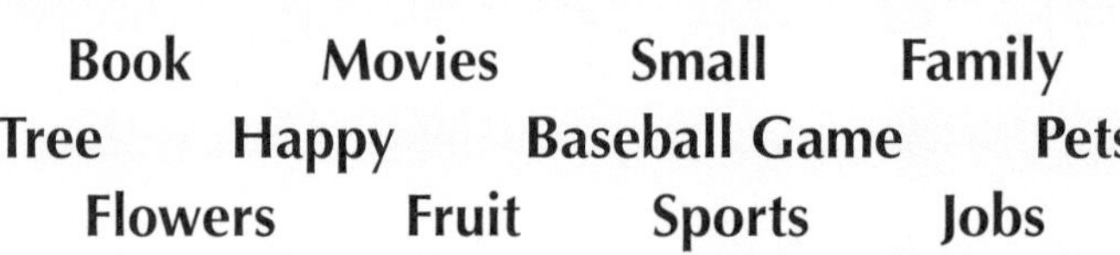

Book Movies Small Family
Tree Happy Baseball Game Pets
Flowers Fruit Sports Jobs

1. **Parts of a** ____________

bark
trunk
root

2. **Names of** ____________

rose
tulip
geranium

3. **Parts of a** ____________

diamond
base
player

4. **Kinds of** ____________

horror
comedy
suspense

5. **Names of** ____________

hamster
dog
canary

6. **Parts of a** ____________

cover
page
word

7. **Parts of a** ____________

mother
father
sister

8. **Words for** ____________

joyful
cheerful
glad

9. **Kinds of** ____________

apple
grapefruit
pineapple

10. **Kinds of** ____________

hockey
soccer
lacrosse

11. **Words for** ____________

little
tiny
miniature

12. **Kinds of** ____________

teacher
mechanic
electrician

You have just witnessed Mia Hamm score the winning goal in a World Cup Soccer match. You would really like to have her come and speak to your class about succeeding in life and in sports.

D. Write a letter of invitation to Mia. Be sure to include all the important information.

__Erosion__ is an important part of the rock cycle. It helps to make a sandy beach, topsoil, and new sedimentary rocks.

A. You are given "before" and "after" scenes. Choose the most likely cause of the change or erosion from the list of possible answers. Write the letters.

Possible Causes of Erosion

A. plant roots grow in cracks, and grow larger
B. dragged along, slowly but surely, by a glacier
C. large amounts of fast flowing water
D. battered by wind-blown sand
E. tumbled with other rocks through water

	Before	After	Cause
1.	sharp edged rock	smooth rounded stone	
2.	enormous boulder	deposited a long distance away	
3.	rock with small cracks	rock broken to pieces	
4.	small stream of water	deep canyon	
5.	rock cliffs by a sandy shore with a house atop the cliff	rock cliffs worn smooth, with cliff edge closer to the house	

B. In each picture, what can you add to stop erosion from occurring? Draw them in the pictures.

C. Extreme weather can cause erosion right before your eyes. Unscramble these words to reveal land-changing events.

1. dofol ________________
2. sladdenli ________________
3. danoort ________________
4. queratheak ________________
5. morst ________________

D. Try this out with your friends.

Put some soil on one end of an old cake pan. Pack it so that if forms a firm slope up one end of the pan. Most of the pan should be free of soil. Now pour in some water to about one centimetre high. Slowly, move the pan side to side to create waves. Do you see the soil bank eroding?

Week 6

SOCIAL STUDIES

Some castles go back as far as the 9th century. Read the passage about castles and then label the castle on the next page.

Castles

Castles were held together with mortar and had **walls** as thick as 30 feet! A castle had many underground passages as well as a drawbridge, a moat, a sentry walk, the inner and outer bailey, and gatehouses.

Castles were often built on high mountains, surrounded by a **moat**. They had a **drawbridge** over the moat that could be raised when enemies came to attack.

The walls of a castle had small slits in them, built for arrows to be shot out at the enemy. They were called **arrow loops**. Defenders of the castle also stood on **ledges** on the top of the castle, which had round walls.

The attackers used **catapults**, crossbows, and lighted arrows. They also used battering rams to knock down walls.

1.
2.
3.
4.
5.
6.

Materials:

- medium googly eyes
- corn kernel
- red yarn
- brown or black felt piece
- "hair" yarn in appropriate colour for Dad
- florist wire or thin black pipe cleaner
- walnut (broken in half – take out nut)
- hot glue gun
- 2 small sunflower seeds
- magnetic strip
- newspaper

Directions:

1. Break walnut in half. Clean inside.
2. Glue googly eyes with hot glue gun.
3. Glue corn kernel "nose".
4. Glue red yarn for mouth.
5. Glue seeds on sides for ears.
6. Twist florist wire into glasses, if your dad wears glasses.
7. Stuff back of walnut with newspaper.
8. Glue felt piece to walnut back.
9. Glue magnetic strip to back.
10. Glue on yarn "hair".

A. **Mr. Brown is a park-keeper. He needs some signs for the park. Help him do the division to find how much each type of sign costs.**

1. 4 signs for $552

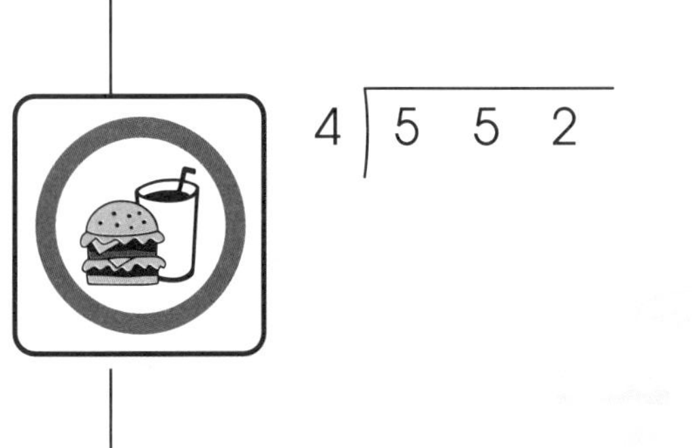

$4 \overline{)\ 5\ \ 5\ \ 2}$

Each costs $ ______ .

2. 5 signs for $795

Each costs $ ______ .

3. 9 signs for $819

Each costs $ ______ .

4. 6 signs for $744

Each costs $ ______ .

5. 8 signs for $696

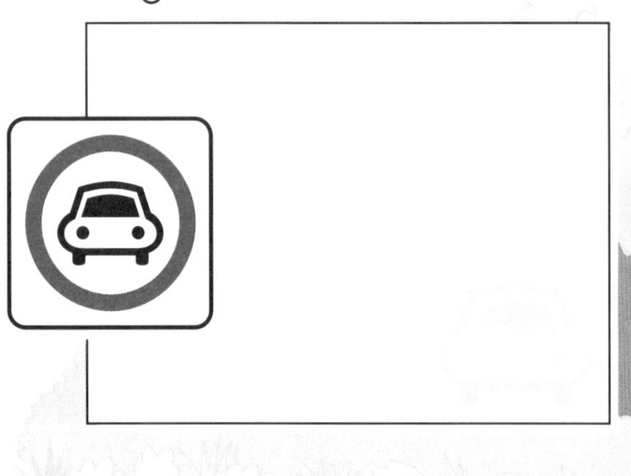

Each costs $ ______ .

6. 3 signs for $159

Each costs $ ______ .

Week 7

MATHEMATICS

B. Look at the different views of the structures in the park. Identify their shapes and write the names of the shapes on the lines.

1. Dinosaur Discovery Trail : ____________________

Front view *Side view* *Top view*

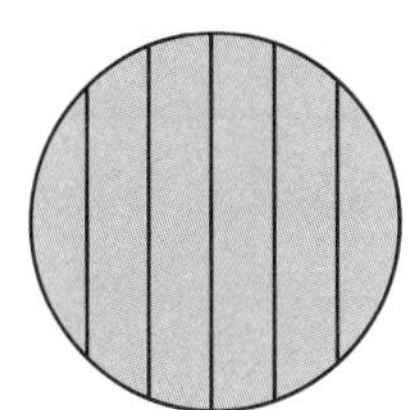

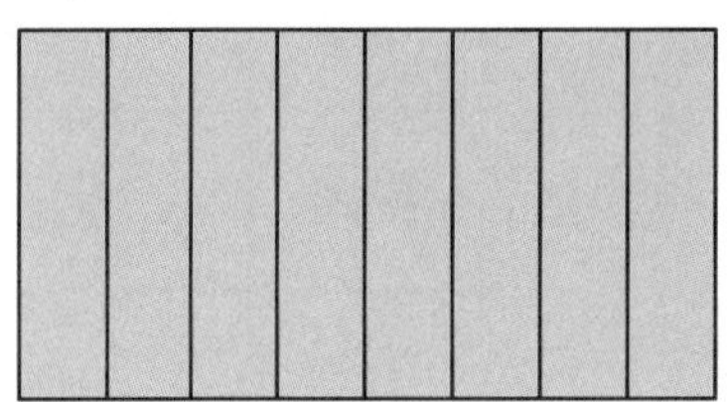

2. Goldfish World : ____________________

Front view *Side view* *Top view*

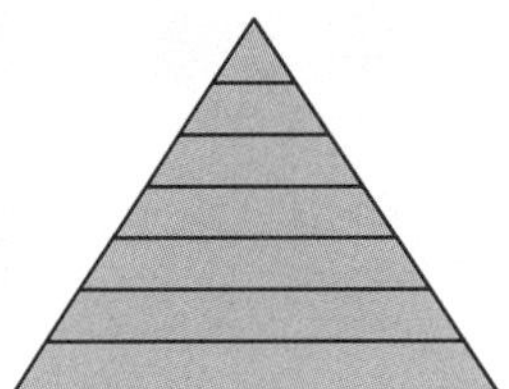
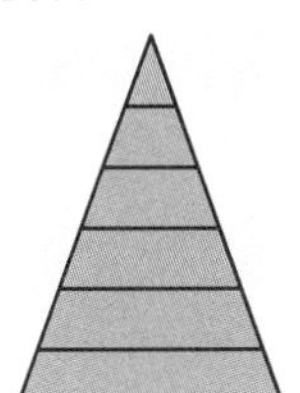
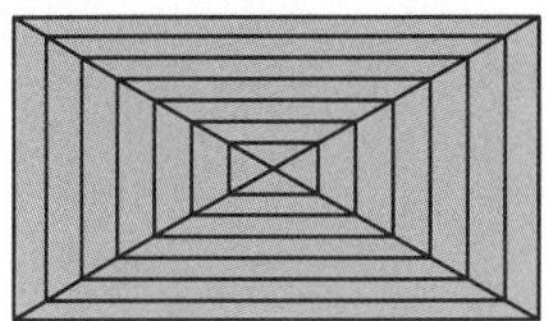

3. Shark Aquarium : ____________________

Front view *Side view* *Top view*

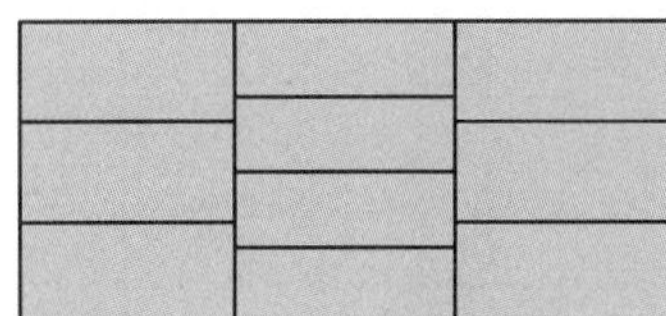

4. Seaview Café : ____________________

Front view *Side view* *Top view*

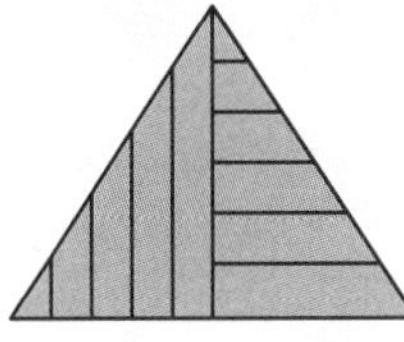

C. **Mr. Brown records the number of visitors to the park last week. Help him complete the table and use the rounded numbers to complete the graph.**

Day	No. of Adults	No. of Children	Total No. of Visitors	Rounded to the Nearest 100
Sun	1653	3315		
Mon	2278	728		
Tue	1653	828		
Wed	2087	1372		
Thu	1554	1409		
Fri	2865	1112		
Sat	3991	1492		

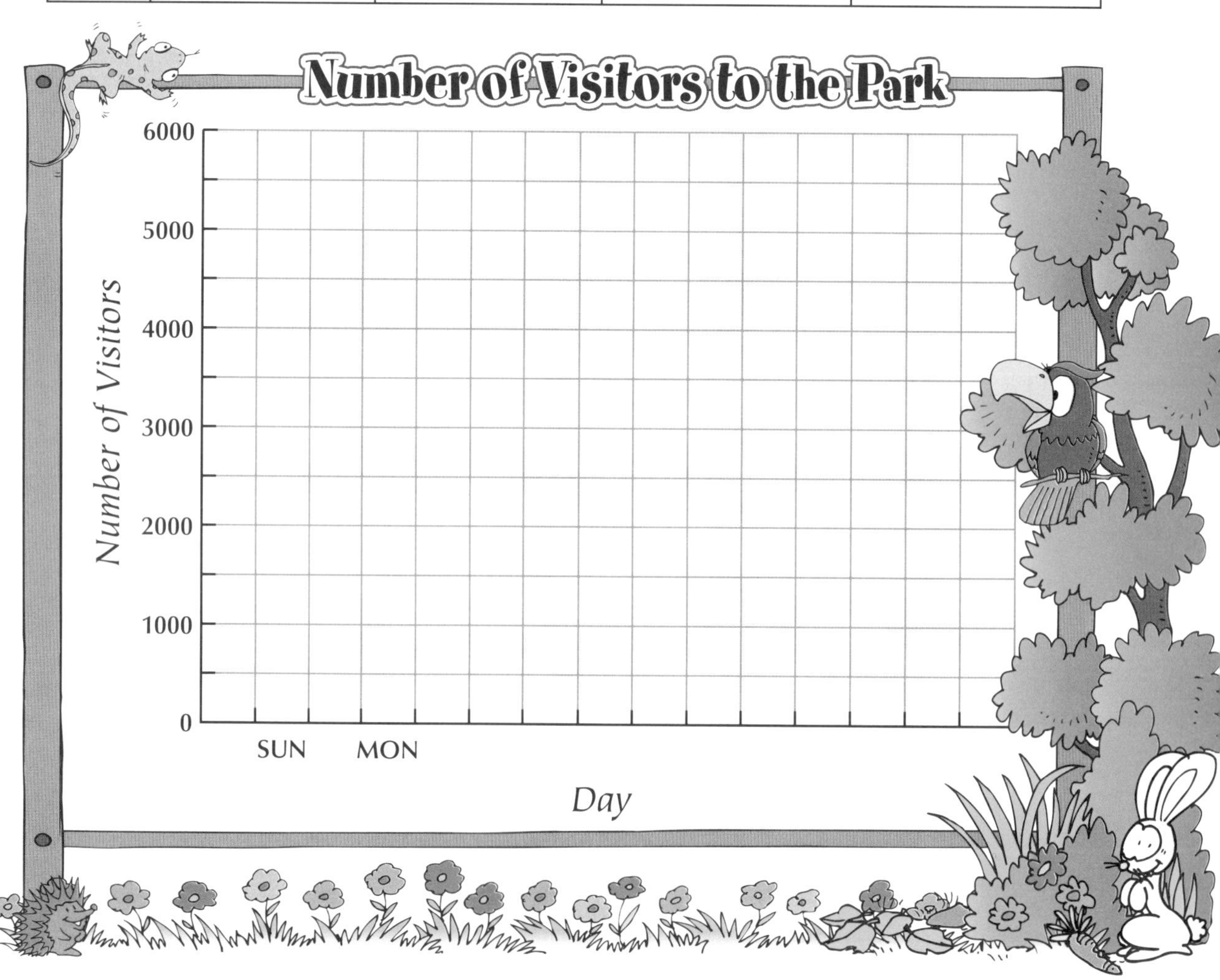

D. Look at the graph again. Answer Mr. Brown's questions.

1. What is the title of the bar graph?

   ____

2. What is the label of the vertical axis?

   ____

3. What is the label of the horizontal axis?

   ____

4. What is the range of the number of visitors?

   ____

5. In multiples of what number is the vertical scale of the graph?

   ____

6. On which days did 4000 or more people visit the park?

   ____

There were 576 rides per day on the Ferris wheel for the first 5 days last week. There were 623 rides per day for the next 2 days. How many rides were there in all last week?

There were __________ rides in all last week.

Pok-a-Tok

When imagining going to a stadium for a big game, visions of hot dogs, popcorn, cheering, and players in team uniforms probably come to mind. Thousands of years ago, the atmosphere on a Mayan playing field in Mexico was much the same, except for one thing. If a team lost, then a human sacrifice was performed. It was usually the captain or coach of the losing team!

In the Mayan game of Pok-a-Tok, there were two teams of seven players. All the players were members of the nobility and the spectators were people from all classes.

Archaeologists have found over 600 ball courts of varying shapes and sizes in Mexico. All of the courts have two sloping walls facing each other with three round disks that probably served as nets of some kind. It seems that the object of the game was for players to keep a ball in the air using every part of the body except the hands.

Ancient Mesoamericans loved a good show. The ballplayers walked onto the court wearing fine jewellery, animal skins, and feathered headdresses. However, during the game, they wore protective gear that allowed for quick movement. The ball was usually made from a human skull wrapped with strips of rubber from the native rubber tree. This made for a very bouncy ball. It usually weighed as much as an average-sized watermelon. The ball had the ability to break bones or even kill!

The Mesoamericans believed that by playing this game correctly, they were serving their gods well. In return, they believed that the gods would provide bountiful crops and good health for their people.

A. Answer the following questions.

1. What is the major difference between a ball game during Mayan times and the ones we go to today?

____

2. What evidence do we have that Pok-a-Tok was a popular game among the Mesoamerican people?

____

3. What did the players wear as they entered the court?

____

4. Why was it important that the players be able to move quickly?

____

5. How was the game ball made?

____

6. Why was the game of Pok-a-Tok so important to the Mesoamerican people?

____

B. The following sentences are not true. Write the true sentences on the lines.

1. In a Pok-a-Tok ball court, there are three baskets on the two straight walls.

____

2. The Pok-a-Tok players wore fine jewellery during the game to show off their wealth.

____

3. The captain or coach of the losing team would perform a sacrifice by killing a lamb.

____

C. Read the clues and complete the crossword puzzle with words from the passage.

Across

A. preventing something from harm
B. plenty of
C. local
D. where people watch sports
E. people watching an event

Down

1. upper class
2. people who studies things of the past
3. offering to a god
4. of the distant past

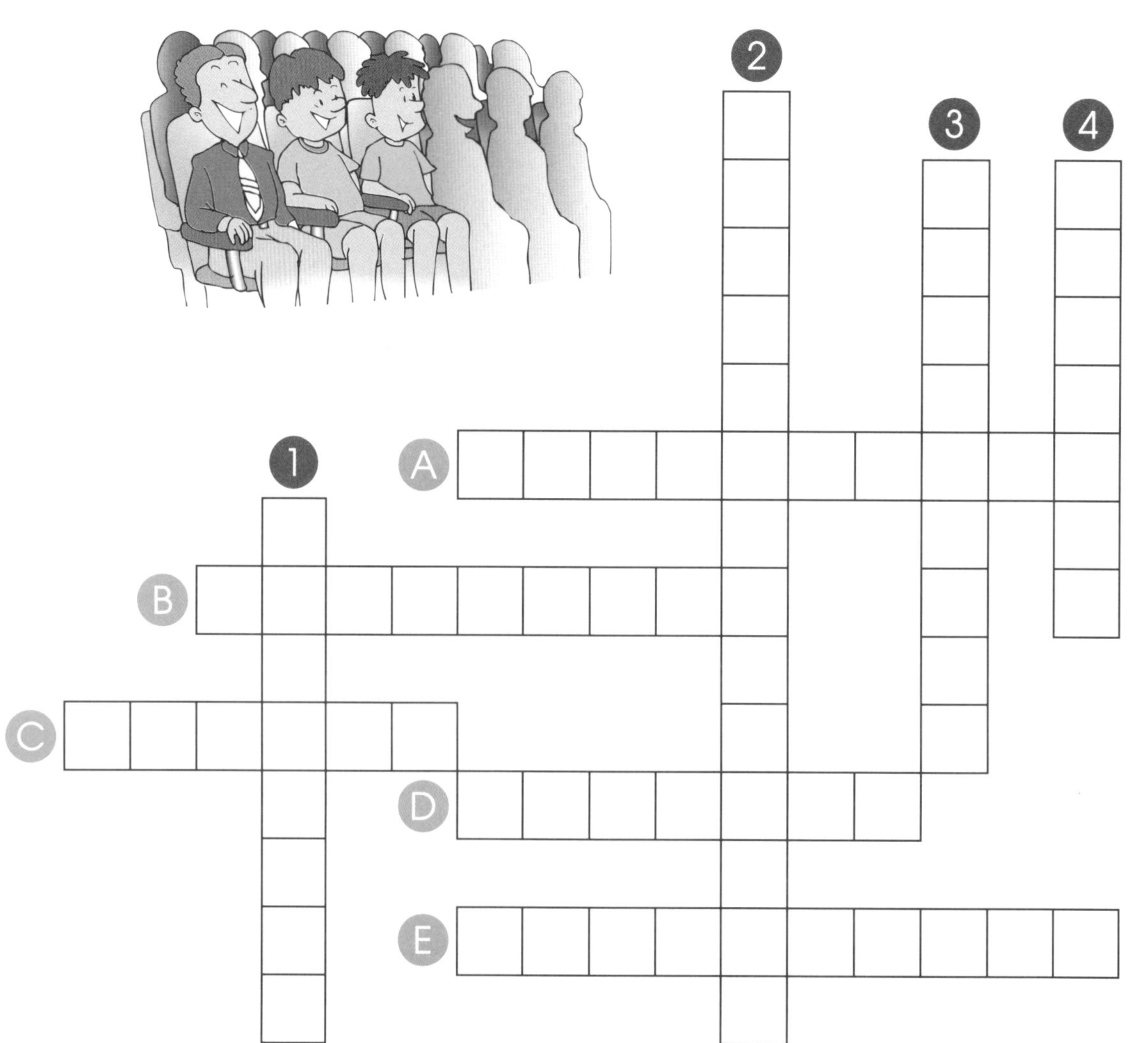

Week 7 ENGLISH

D. Using the Venn Diagram, list two ways in which Pok-a-Tok is different from basketball and two ways the two sports are similar.

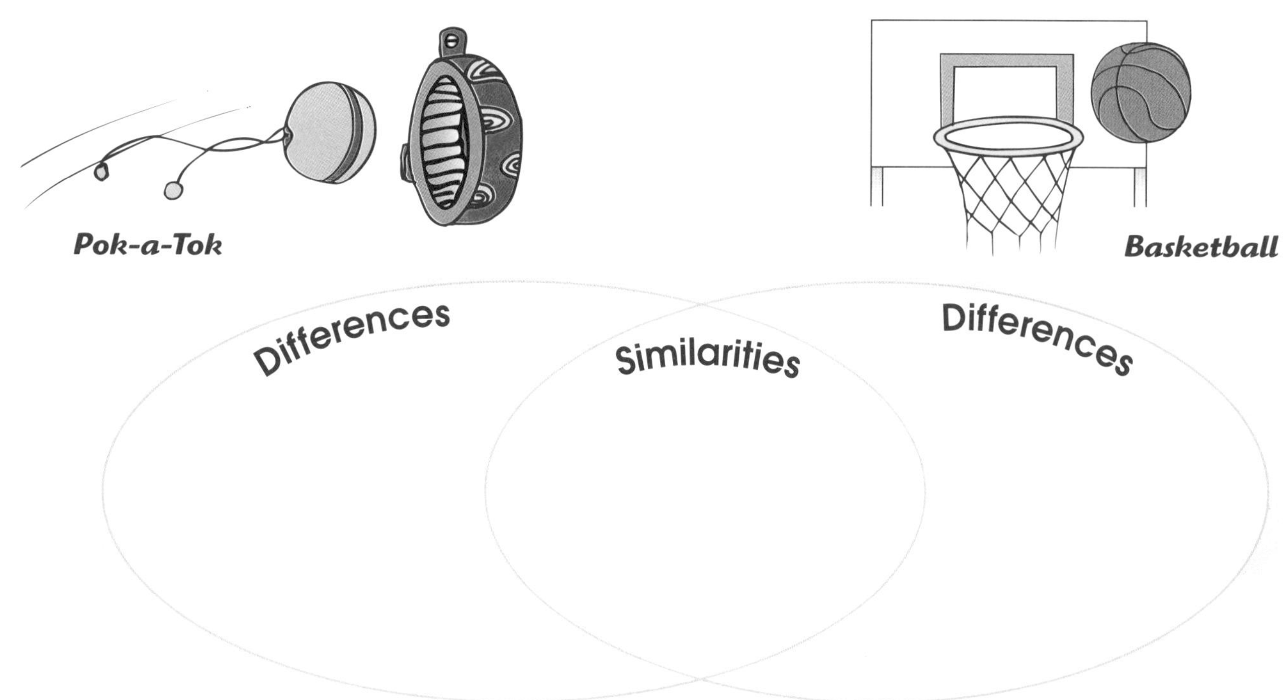

E. Write a paragraph describing how a game of basketball is played.

Human *Body Systems*

A. Ninjo and his one-eyed brother are writing a report of their research on the human body systems. Help them complete the table.

Body System

Nervous
Circulatory
Respiratory
Skeletal
Digestive
Excretory

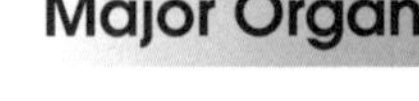

Major Organ

Kidney
Bone
Brain
Lung
Heart
Stomach

Body System	Major Organ	Function
1. ________ System	2. ________	Controls the body's responses to internal and external stimuli
3. ________ System	4. ________	Responsible for the ingestion, digestion, and absorption of food
5. ________ System	6. ________	Supports and protects the body
7. ________ System	8. ________	Removes waste from the body
9. ________ System	10. ________	Delivers nutrients to cells and removes waste
11. ________ System	12. ________	Exchange of oxygen and carbon dioxide between the body and the environment

B. Find the following "body" words in the word search.

One of the most remarkable inventions of the Middle Ages was the printing press. The first printed book, the Bible, was produced in 1455.

A. Many things changed after the invention of the printing press. Read the statements below and check "Before" or "After".

	Before	After
1. Books were made mainly in monasteries.	______	______
2. Few people could read.	______	______
3. Books were written by hand.	______	______
4. Letters could be put together and printed as words.	______	______
5. Books became cheaper to produce.	______	______
6. The Bible is the most popular book.	______	______
7. Libraries grew; more people could read.	______	______
8. Communication became easier.	______	______
9. The number of people who read increased.	______	______
10. The Chinese printed using wooden blocks.	______	______

By the time Gutenberg introduced printing to Europe in the mid-15th century, the Chinese had been developing the process for nearly 1000 years.

B. Read the statements below and decide whether these things happened only then, only now, or both. Write "then", "now", or "both" respectively.

1. Towns and cities have garbage and sewage everywhere.

2. People travel long distances quickly.

3. Most people live in families.

4. Kings and queens have all the power.

5. People die if they get an infection.

6. Some people live on the streets.

7. Men and women do the same jobs.

8. Explorers use ships to find new lands.

9. Poor people fight for rights.

10. Children work at the same jobs as adults.

11. People go on pilgrimages.

12. If you are born poor, you stay poor.

Medieval Costumes

Materials:

- bristol board
- long ribbons
- hot glue gun
- coloured paper
- pencil
- scissors

Knight's Helmet

Materials:

- grey paint
- hot glue gun
- coloured paper
- scissors
- bristol board
- hole punch
- 4 elastic bands
- sponge or fabric rag

Lady's Hat

Directions:

1. Shape bristol board into semi-circle to make cone.
2. Make a cone with pointy top.
3. Decorate hat with coloured paper.
4. Cut lengths of ribbon.
5. Hot glue ribbon at top.

Directions:

1. Measure your head (top to chin).
2. Draw 2 shapes on to bristol board using length measured. Cut out.
3. Cut out ovals for eyes and mouth from front piece.
4. Rub grey paint with sponge or rag over front and back. Let dry.
5. Decorate helmet with coloured paper.
6. Punch 2 holes on both sides of each piece.
7. Cut 4 elastic bands. Pull them through holes on front and back as shown and tie knots.

A. **The children are making flowers with paper. Look at the flowers. Help them draw the lines of symmetry on the flowers.**

1.

2.

3.

4.

5.

6.

B. See how the children cut the paper flowers. Help them measure the angle of each petal. Then answer the questions.

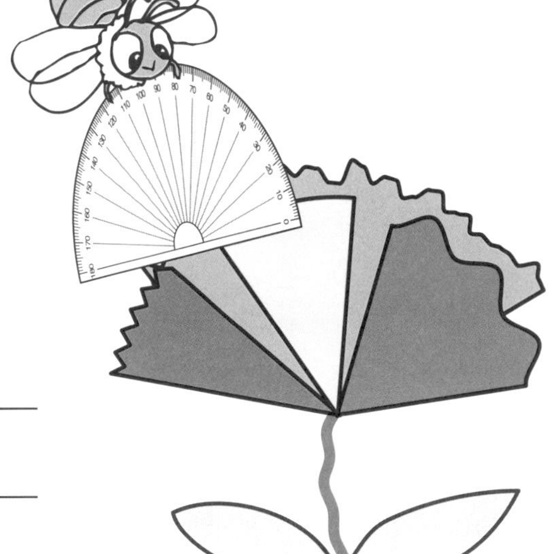

1.

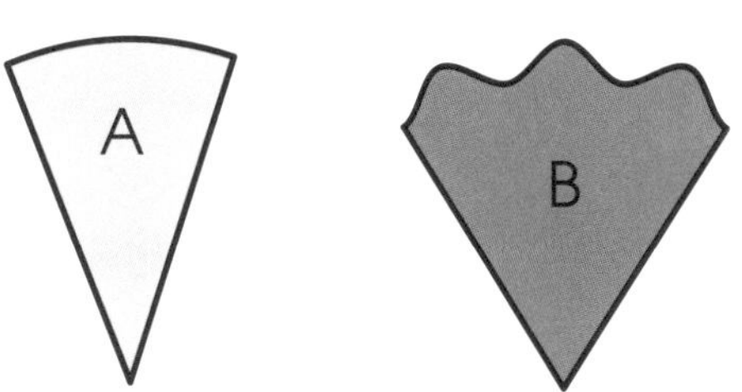

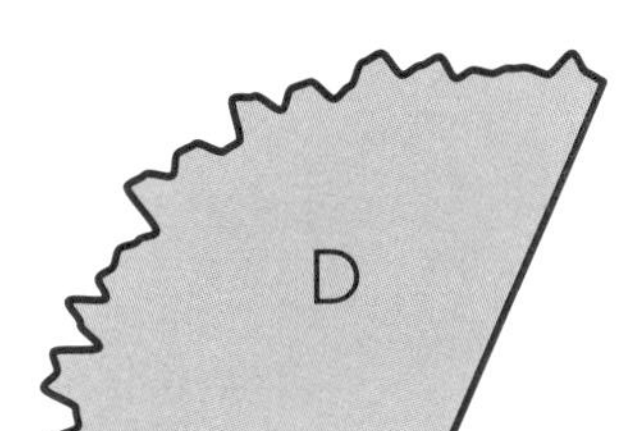

A. ________

B. ________

C. ________

D. ________

2.

Mabel uses 5 paper petals to make 1 flower. If she has 231 paper petals, how many flowers can she make?

____________ = ________   ______ flowers

3.

If a stem is 8 cm long, how many stems can Ivy make with a piece of wire 850 mm long?

____________ = ________   ______ stems

4.

Each flower has 2 leaves. If Winnie makes 108 flowers, how many leaves does she need?

____________ = ________   ______ leaves

C. **Find how long it has taken each girl to make 50 paper flowers. Then answer the questions.**

Mabel

Start **Finish**

Ivy

Start **Finish**

Winnie

Start **Finish**

Stella

Start **Finish**

1.

Time Taken

Mabel :	min	Ivy :	min
Winnie :	min	Stella :	min

2. Who has taken the longest time? ______________

3. Who has taken the shortest time? ______________

4. Winnie took a 6-minute break when she was making the flowers. If Winnie had not taken any rest, at what time would she have finished? ______________

D. Each girl uses sticks and marshmallows to show the shape of her vase. Check ✔ the correct letter to tell the shape of each vase.

1\.

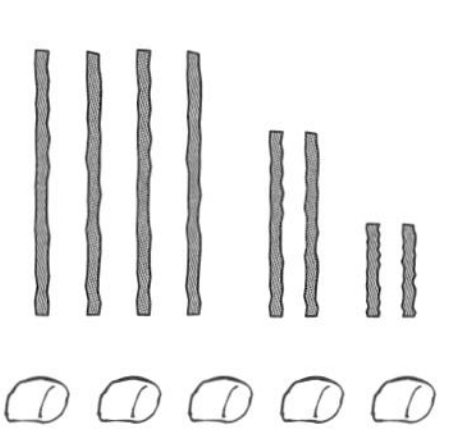

Ⓐ 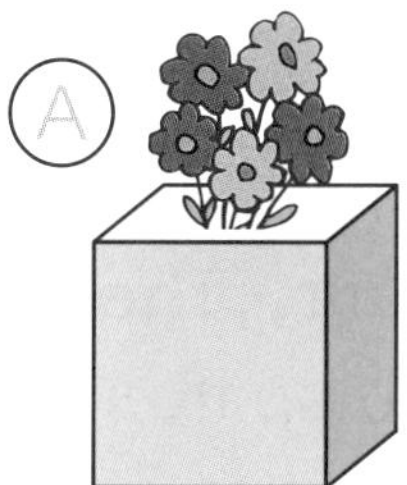

Ⓑ 

Ⓒ 

2\.

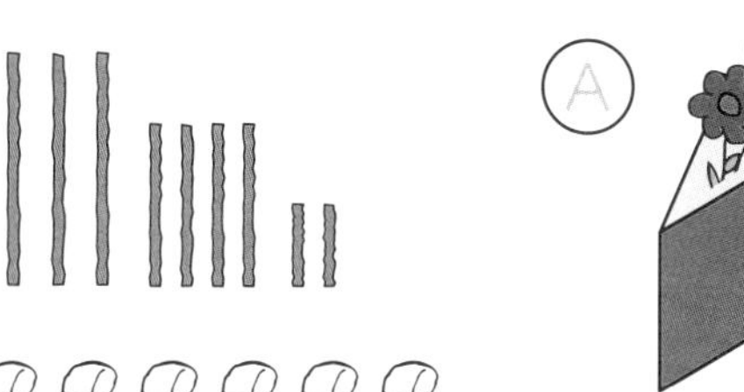

Ⓑ 

Ⓒ 

3\.

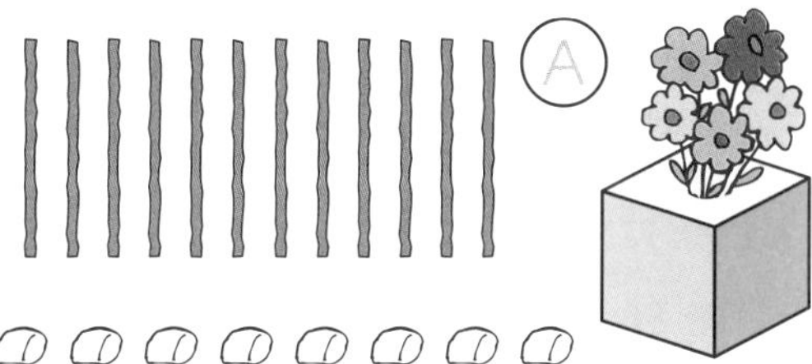

Ⓑ 

Ⓒ 

Look at the diagram. Answer the question.

What is the smallest number of toothpicks you can remove in order to have exactly 5 squares left?

________ toothpick(s) can be removed.

Dear Diary

Dear Diary,

We just moved here to our new home in Canada. I am so excited to be living in this beautiful country. It is the first day of spring. The grass is turning a lush green colour. The tulips in the flowerbeds are poking out their heads, just waking up from their winter's sleep.

The children in the neighbourhood are riding their bicycles. In the park, people are walking their dogs, inhaling the fresh spring air. I know that I am going to love this country. Summer is around the corner and I can hardly wait to experience a truly Canadian summer.

Dear Diary,

Today is the first day of summer. I love Canada more and more each day. The days seem longer and it is very hot outside. All of the gardens are in full bloom and the shade of the trees is a welcoming sight.

I have made some new friends here and our favourite activity is running through the sprinkler. I have learned to play baseball and my rollerblading is getting better each day. I understand that fall will bring a reprieve from the heat and I can't wait to see what else comes with this season.

Dear Diary,

Today is the first day of fall. I think that Canada is the most beautiful place on Earth. The leaves have turned many shades of red, yellow, and orange. I went for a ride through the majestic countryside and saw some deer darting into the forest.

My friends and I get together to help each other rake leaves. We make a huge pile and have a terrific time frolicking in the leaves. Next week, I am going on a hayride and then we will have a bonfire in the woods. I can't imagine what surprises are in store for me this winter. I can hardly wait to see snow for the first time.

A. List three things that the writer had not done before moving to Canada.

1. ____________________

2. ____________________

3. ____________________

B. Pretend you are the author of this diary and write the diary entry for winter. Keep in mind that you have never seen snow before. Use descriptive language to paint a picture of the things you see and experience.

Dear Diary,

Today is the first day of winter. I could hardly believe my eyes when I looked out my window this morning. ____________________

C. **Read the clues and complete the crossword puzzle with words from the diary.**

Across		**Down**	
A.	great	1.	impressive
B.	feel	2.	making a sudden movement
C.	typically	3.	having fun
D.	breathing in	4.	relief
		5.	rich growth

Week 8

ENGLISH

D. An antonym is a word that means the opposite of another word. Circle one antonym for each word listed below.

1.	beautiful	attractive	ugly	striking	smart
2.	fresh	clean	bright	stale	new
3.	huge	gigantic	massive	large	tiny
4.	hot	scorching	warm	cold	humid
5.	first	last	early	second	start
6.	arrive	appear	leave	land	enter
7.	outside	outdoors	nature	beyond	inside
8.	friend	buddy	pal	stranger	chum

E. Use the information from the diary entries to fill in the missing words below.

1. In spring, the grass is ______________ , tulips are in ______________ , and people like to take their dogs on long ______________ .

2. In summer, it is very ______________ outside. The ______________ of the trees offers a place to cool off. ______________ through the sprinkler is a fun activity.

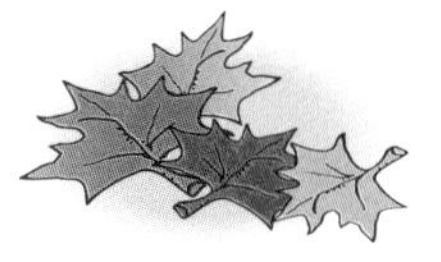

3. In the fall, the leaves turn ______________ of red, yellow, and orange. We enjoy ______________ in the huge ______________ of leaves.

Climate is the average weather patterns of an area year after year. Weather is what the atmosphere brings us daily, and even within a day.

Weather & Climate

Week 8

SCIENCE

A. Some of these statements are considering what the climate of an area is. Others are considering the weather. Write "climate" or "weather" for each sentence.

1. Manitoba has cold winters and warm, sunny summers. ____________________

2. It's raining today. Get your umbrella. ____________________

3. Plant your garden after a rainfall, when the soil is moist. ____________________

4. Ontario's Niagara Peninsula is a good place to grow grapes. ____________________

5. The dark clouds moving in indicate a storm is coming. ____________________

6. Desert plants grow in B.C.'s Okanagan Valley.

   ____

7. Here, we use bricks to build our homes.

   ____

8. We're moving to Vancouver Island! Let's make sure we all have umbrellas.

   ____

B. Complete the crossword puzzle with weather words.

Across

A. snow, rain, sleet, or hail
B. the condensation of water vapour on the earth, usually overnight
C. the study of the atmosphere and what goes on inside it
D. refers to water vapour held in the air

Word Bank

WINDCHILL
DEW
HUMIDITY
CLOUD
HEAT
METEOROLOGY
FOG
PRECIPITATION
WIND
EVAPORATION

Down

1. energy produced by the sun
2. water vapour condensed to tiny drops of water
3. Water disappears into the air by this process.
4. a cloud at ground level
5. moving air
6. considering the effect of wind as well as temperature

Science Fun

Hail is the result of bits of ice being tossed up and down through storm clouds, gaining layers and getting bigger the longer their ride is.

The largest hail stone ever reported was about the size of a softball!

A. Medieval towns developed as people moved from the manors and settled in one place. Circle the correct letter to complete each sentence.

1. Most medieval towns were ____ .

   A. large B. small C. middle-sized

2. Many towns began as places where people gathered for ____ .

   A. praying B. schooling C. fairs

3. Being located near water was important for ____ .

   A. food B. transportation C. entertainment

4. The town market was a place where ____ was/were sold.

   A. produce B. horses C. paper

5. Most of the townspeople were ____ .

   A. peasants B. craftsmen C. merchants

6. Part of the attraction of towns was the ____ .

   A. freedom B. excitement C. peaceful atmosphere

7. One thing that all medieval towns and cities had was a ____ .

   A. town hall B. fire station C. church

8. There was no ____ in a medieval town.

   A. poverty B. law C. sewage system

Cathedrals began to be built in the 12th century.

B. There were many people involved in building a cathedral. Look at the jobs described below. Write the representing letters in the correct boxes.

- (A) Shaped the blocks of stones and set them into place.
- (B) Built the construction scaffolding and put up the roof.
- (C) Drew designs for windows and cut small pieces of glass.
- (D) Decorated archways and pillars with saints, angels, flowers, and leaves.
- (E) Cut the beams, rafters, and frames.
- (F) Bound together pieces of glass with strips of lead.
- (G) Created elaborate designs of animals and faces in wood.
- (H) Carved stone figures called gargoyles.

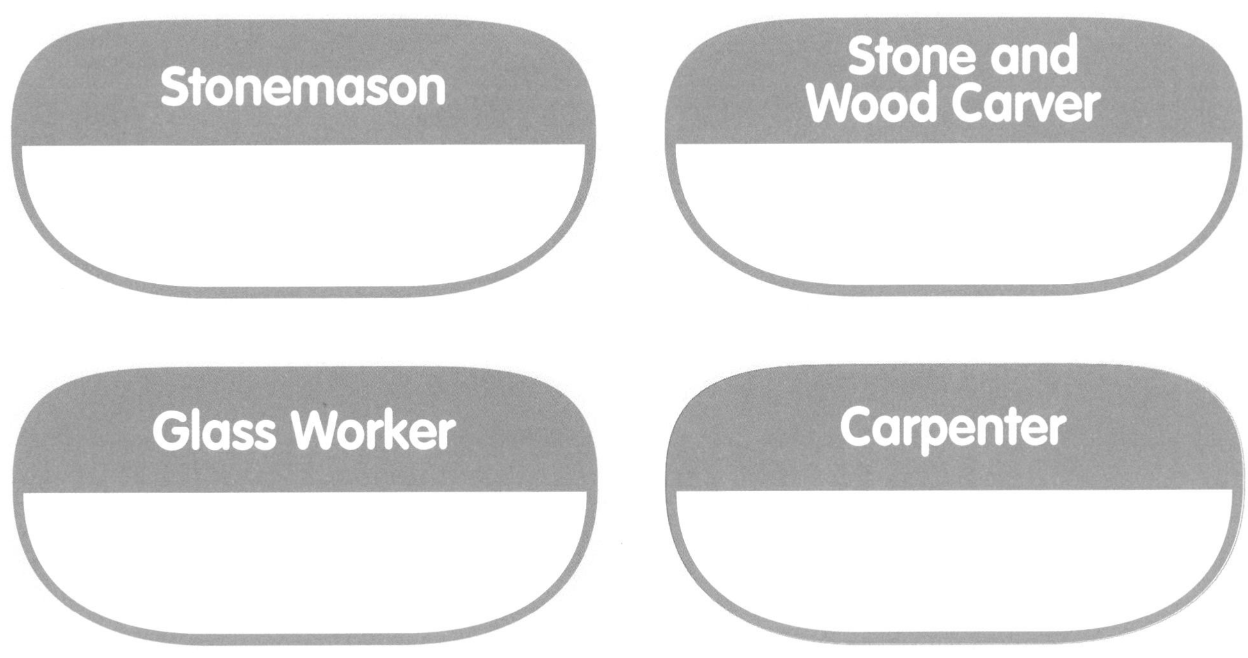

Week 8

ARTS & CRAFTS

Medieval Shield

Materials:

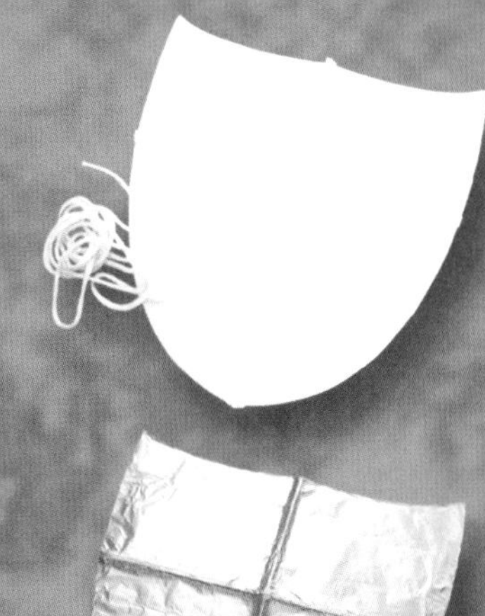

- 1 large sheet of bristol board
- several large sheets of aluminum foil
- black paint
- sponge
- styrofoam tray
- pencil
- string and glue
- masking tape
- scissors

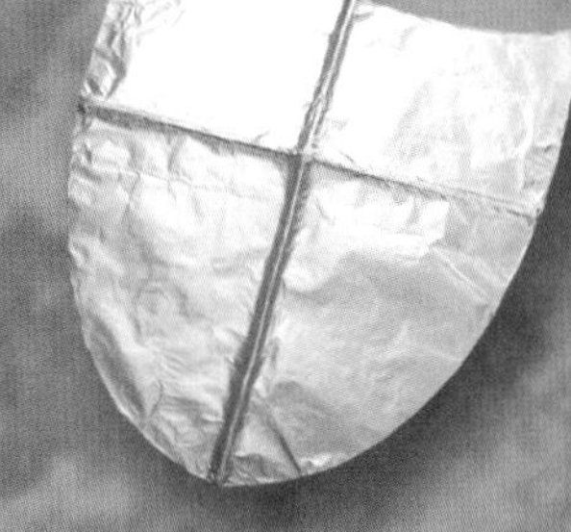

Directions:

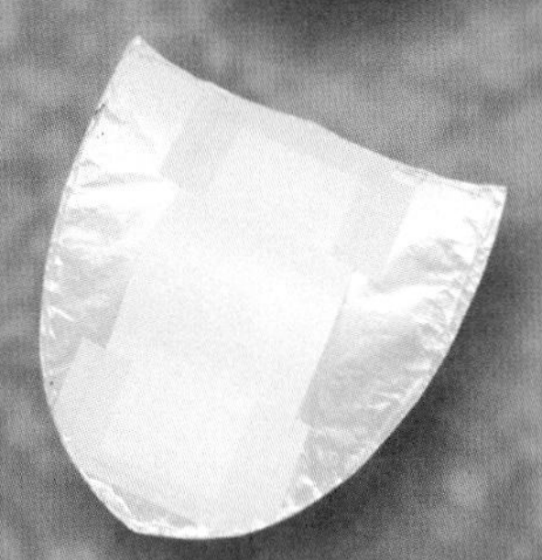

1. Draw a shield on bristol board. Cut out.
2. Dip string into glue and "draw" vertical and horizontal lines. Let dry.
3. Cover shield with aluminum foil, pressing around the string lines.
4. Dip sponge into black paint on styrofoam tray and sponge over shield (dabbing). Let dry.
5. Go over wrinkled and creased areas a second time. Let dry.
6. Cut a small handle out of bristol board and tape to back of shield.

ANSWERS

Week 1

Mathematics

A. 1. 19.50
2. 10.80
3. 13.20
4. 16.50
5. Chips, Pizza, Popcorn, Chocolates
6. Chocolates
7. $30.30
8. $60

B. 1. 124 ; 620
2. 2000 ; 1450
3. a. 400 b. 120 c. 5
4. a. 2 ; 2000 b. 200 c. 2000 ; 2

C. 1. a. Henry b. Elaine c. Ray d. Ray ; Henry
2. a. David b. Suzy c. Tim d. David ; Suzy
3. a. Alex b. Sean c. Gloria d. Sean ; Gloria

D. 1. 1450
2. 173
3. 97

Brain Teaser

20

English

A. 1. T 2. F 3. F 4. T 5. F 6. T

B. 1. By the age 11 months, he began swinging his own miniature club.
2. Throughout his career...his positive attitude sees him through these experiences.
3. Despite the flashes...he continues to maintain his concentration.
4. Apart from...qualities that make him a dominating force in the world of golf.
5. At the age of 21...ended the year winning a total of $790 594.

C.

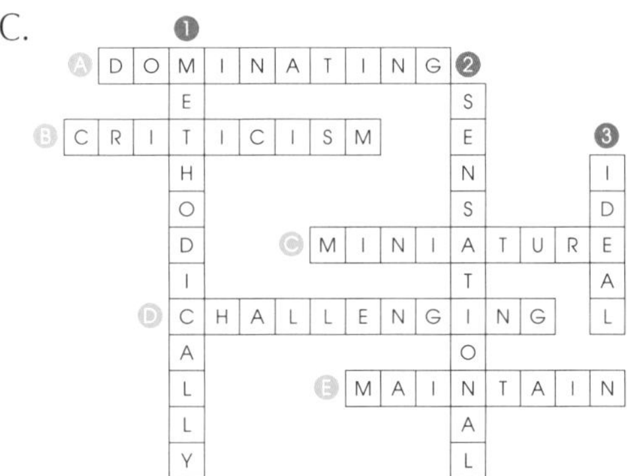

D. 1. ? ; A 2. . ; T
3. . ; I 4. ! ; E
5. ! ; E

E. (Individual writing)

Science

A. 1. beaver
2. preying mantis
3. viceroy butterfly
4. wood frog
5. polar bear
6. wolf
7. white fox

B. 1. B 2. E 3. A 4. D 5. C 6. F

Social Studies

A. 1. Innuitian Region
2. Arctic Lowlands
3. Canadian Shield
4. Cordilleran Region
5. Hudson Bay Lowlands
6. Appalachian Region
7. Interior Plains
8. St. Lawrence Lowlands

B. 1. B 2. B
3. A 4. C
5. A 6. C

Challenge

1. C
2. Superior, Michigan, Huron, Erie, Ontario

Week 2

Mathematics

A. A : 0.5 B : 1.2
   C : 3 D: 5.2
   E : 7

B. 1. 69 2. 74
   3. 143 ; 2 ; 23

C. 1. 2 ; 0.8 ; $\frac{8}{10}$
   2. 0.4 ; $\frac{4}{10}$; 0.6 ; $\frac{6}{10}$
   3. 0.7 ; $\frac{7}{10}$; 0.3 ; $\frac{3}{10}$
   4. 0.15 ; $\frac{15}{100}$; 0.45 ; $\frac{45}{100}$; 0.4 ; $\frac{40}{100}$

D. 1. 65 2. 80
   3. 95 4. 110
   5. 8 6. 11
   7. Each blade of grass is 15 mm longer than the previous one.
   8. 125 9. 920

E. 1. 5 m
   2. 15 cm
   3. 2 km^2
   4. 36 m^2

Math Game

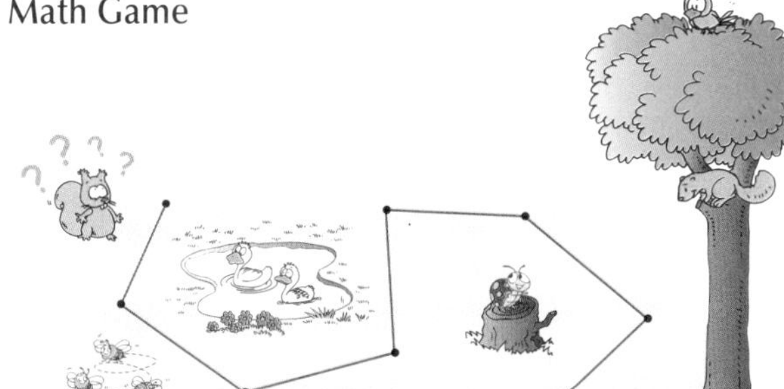

English

A. 1. transportation
   2. expeditions
   3. construction
   4. sensitive
   5. recreation

B. Kayaks of the Past
   Design : frame made from driftwood and whalebones ; animal skins stretched over the frame ; ranged in width
   Uses : mainly used on hunting expeditions for caribou and seals
   Kayaks of the Present
   Design : made from fibreglass or strong plastics ; partitions, leg braces, and footrests added
   Uses : mainly used for recreation and sport

C. 1. wore
   2. found
   3. drank
   4. rode
   5. ran
   6. gave
   7. sang
   8. broke
   9. drew
   10. bought

D. 1. rode
   2. bought
   3. gave
   4. broke
   5. found
   6. wore
   7. ran
   8. sang
   9. drank
   10. drew

E. <u>summor</u> ; summer
   <u>their</u> ; there
   <u>beleive</u> ; believe
   <u>approched</u> ; approached
   <u>mite</u> ; might
   <u>it's</u> ; its

F. 1. Before we go kayaking, we have to put on lifejackets and other protective gear.
   2. The next World Cup series will be in 2010.

Science

A. 1. bald eagle
   2. sow bug
   3. beaver
   4. marmot

B. Pond : duck, fish, mosquito, frog, tadpole
   Tree : caterpillar, bat, beetle, robin, owl
   Soil : mole, worm, groundhog

Social Studies

A.

b	l	e	I	b	s	t	b	h		r	i	o	y	s	e	r
h	y	d	r	o	-	e	l	e	c	t	r	i	c	i	t	y
p	o	t	s	y	p	r	u	h	l	t	n	l	a	o	n	a
r	a	n	h	s	o	z	d	I	c	i	t	y	l	y	h	g
a	j	s	a	t	e	m	o	r	x	b	s	a	l	t	b	e
l	u	m	b	e	r	rt	-	i	p	l	a	m	u	o	p	a
t	r	d		r	q	b	e		l	s	l	t	m	e	o	t
i	b	f	i	s	h	s	l	m	o	d	o	-	e	l	t	r
h	g	i	e	a	u	a	l	o	b	e	i	v	a	q	a	j
y	I	r	i	s	h		m	o	s	s	f	b	c	o	t	b
d	t	o	g	m	j	d	p	a	t	a	t	e	s	f	o	i
e	t	n	f	l	o	b	l	u	e	b	e	r	r	i	e	s
b	e	r	r	u	s	a	m	I	r	p	l	i		m	s	h
g	r	n	r	o	-	l	o	e	s	h	e	o	i	y	c	d
i	s	e	s	b	f	s	q	l	a	e	c	i	t	t	l	s

fish

B. 1. source
   2. flow
   3. tributary
   4. mouth
   5. branch
   6. delta

C.

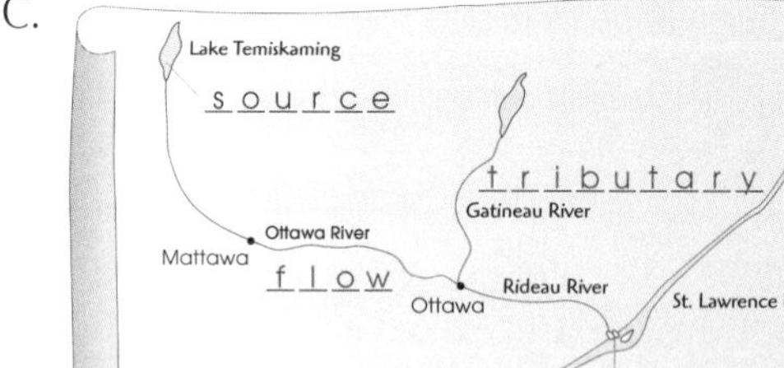

Week 3

Mathematics

A. 1. 38.5 ; 1.48
   2. 39.6 ; 1.53
   3. 36.4 ; 1.37
   4.
   5.

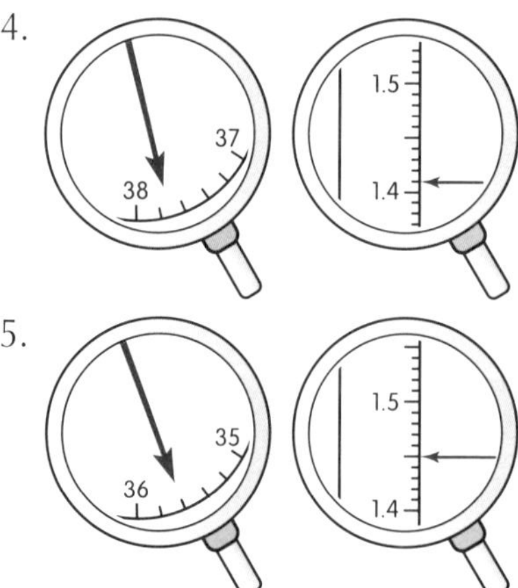

B. 1. 1.53 m ; 1.48 m ; 1.45 m ; 1.41 m ; 1.37 m
   2. 39.6 kg ; 38.5 kg ; 37.7 kg ; 36.4 kg ; 35.6 kg
   3. 38.5 – 36.87 = 1.63 ; 1.63
   4. 1.53 – 1.49 = 0.04 ; 0.04
   5. 1.37 + 0.28 = 1.65 ; 1.65

C. 1.

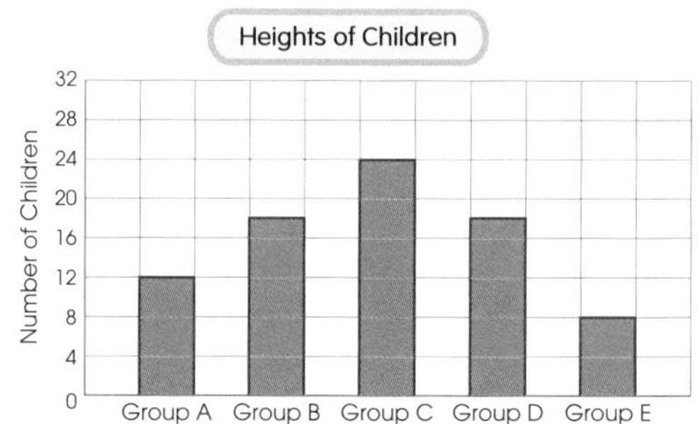

   2. From 110 cm to 119 cm
   3. 18
   4. A

D. 1. 38.5 ; 47.4 ; 8.9 ; 8.9
   2. 1.38 ; 1.54 ; 0.16 ; 0.16

Brain Teaser

Aaron should join the Collectors Club.
He needs to pay : $6.99 + $3x4 = $18.99

English

A. 1. (Suggested answer)
   She enjoys nature, likes speed, and loves dogs.
   2. She went on a trip to Alaska to see the Iditarod Trail race.
   3. Gunther, Rocky, Chinook, and Harley are on her team.
   4. She had them tow her on a mountain bike or in a cart with wheels.

5. (Suggested answer)
   They learn to be endurable and to obey commands.
6. a. pass by something
   b. turn left
   c. start a team
   d. turn right

B. 1. favourite 2. spans
   3. throughout 4. proper
   5. endurance

C. (Individual writing)

D. 1. weak ; week
   2. peak ; peek
   3. two ; too ; to
   4. chilly ; chilli
   5. seen ; scene
   6. heard ; herd

Challenge

(Individual writing)

Science

A. 1. A 2. A
   3. B 4. A
   5. B 6. B

B. 1. candle 2. firefly
   3. kaleidoscope 4. prism
   5. eyeball 6. lightning
   7. transparent 8. shadow

Social Studies

A. 1. Gold 2. Copper
   3. Nickel 4. Lead
   5. Forests 6. Silver
   7. Rivers 8. Fossil fuels

B.

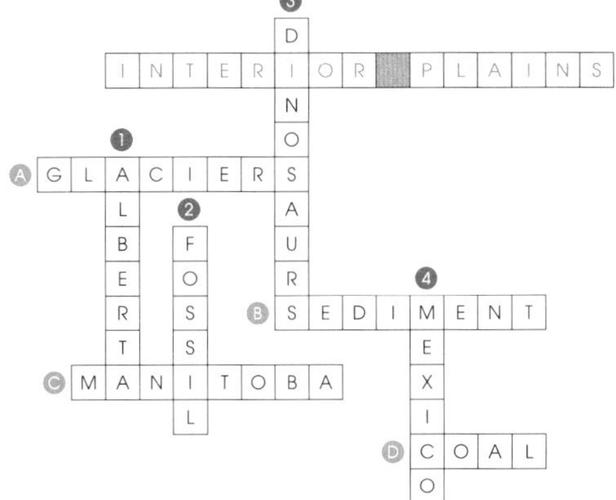

Week 4

Mathematics

A. Quadrilateral

Square :

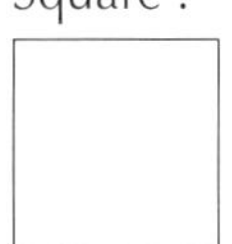

Trapezoid :

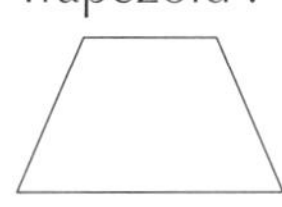

Rectangle :

Rhombus :

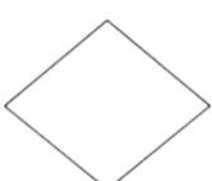

Kite :

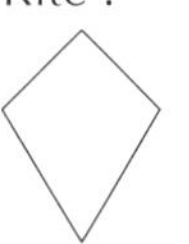

Parallelogram :

Not Quadrilateral

Triangle :

Pentagon :

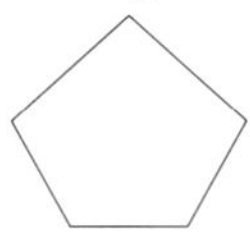

Circle :

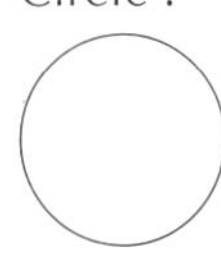

Hexagon :

B. 1. A 2. B
   3. C 4. C

C. 1. ✘ 2. ✔ 3. ✔
   4. ✘ 5. ✔ 6. ✘
   7. ✔ 8. ✔ 9. ✔
   10. ✘

D. 1.  ; 4

2.  ; 2

3. ; 3

4.  ; 1

Math Game

Car : 1.2 ; Soldier : 1.2 ; Piggy bank : 2.4

English

A. 1. T 2. F
3. T 4. T
5. F 6. T
7. F 8. F

B. 1. suds
2. mowing
3. lawn
4. shrink
5. slot
6. grab
7. bright
8. crystals
9. poured
10. found
11. soap
12. spring

C. (Individual writing)

D. 1. bright ; sunny
2. powdered
3. gooey ; yellow
4. bubbly
5. quiet ; peaceful

E. (Individual writing)

F. (Individual drawing)

Science

A. 1. volcano ; igneous ; granite
2. pressure ; metamorphic ; marble
3. sedimentary ; limestone

B. (Individual observation)

C. A, E, F

Social Studies

A.

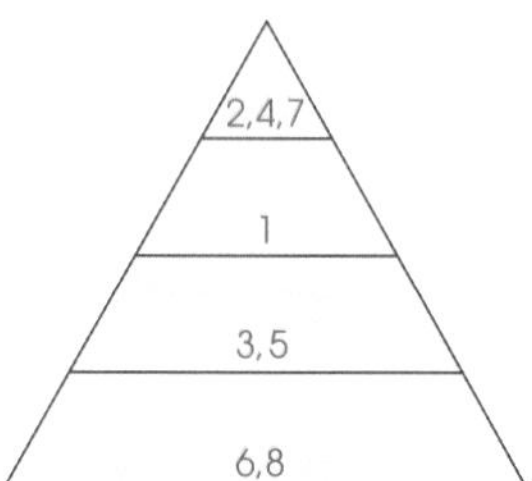

B. 1. A knight
2. The steward, the bailiff, and the reeve
3. a. They paid rent for their land.
b. They had little or no land at all.
c. They paid for their land in services.

Week 5

Mathematics

A. 1. 1903 2. 1953
3. 1933 4. 1783
5. 1462

B. 1. 8 ; 6 ; 2 ; 0
2. 5 ; 1 ; 0 ; 4
3. 6 ; 6 ; 0 ; 0
4. 6 ; 0 ; 1 ; 5
5. 5 ; 3 ; 0 ; 2

C. 1. 14 ; 102 ; 149
2. In 1935 : 1 ; 46 ; 106
In 1985 : 2 ; 18 ; 138
In 2015 : 1 ; 19 ; 79

D. 1.

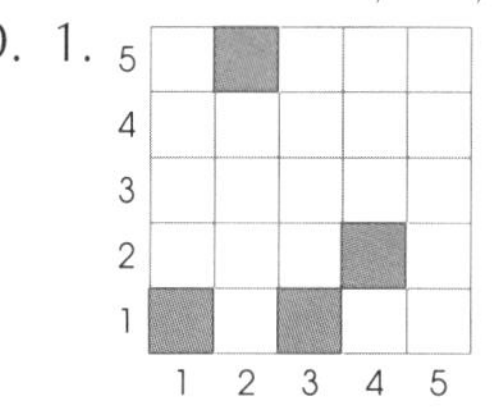

2.

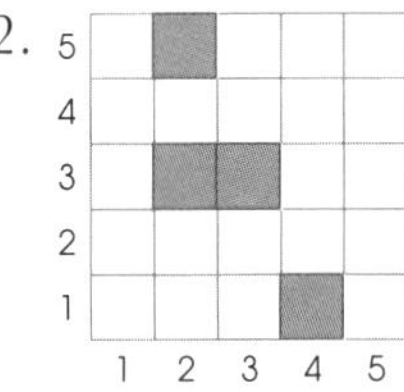

3.

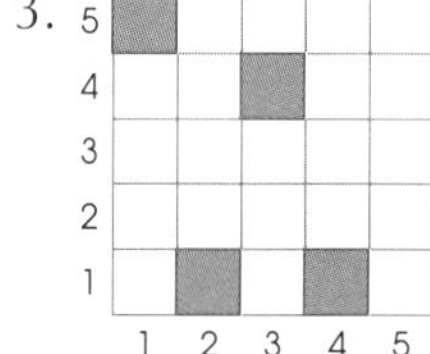

4.

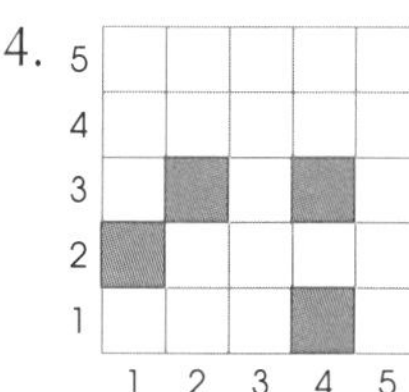

Math Game

1332

English

A. 4 ; 7 ; 2 ; 3 ; 1 ; 5 ; 6

B. 1. accidentally
2. burst
3. experiment
4. scare
5. celebrate
6. Italians
7. timed
8. spectacular

C. 1. loudly
2. quickly
3. in the kitchen
4. to the park
5. every Monday and Wednesday
6. very slowly
7. brightly ; in the night sky
8. soon

D. (Individual writing)

E. (Individual writing)

F. (Individual writing)

Science

A. 1. C 2. B
3. E 4. A
5. D

B. 1. D 2. B
3. C 4. A
5. E

C. 1. D 2. C
3. B 4. A
5. E

Social Studies

A. (Individual answers)

B. 1. knight
2. mother
3. page
4. lord
5. dress
6. armour
7. manor
8. lady
9. squire
10. servant
11. prayed
12. eating
13. sleeping
14. dubbed

Week 6

Mathematics

A. 1. 9.95 + 12.63 = 22.58
He needs to pay $22.58.
2. 21.65 + 5.62 = 27.27
Edward does not have enough money to buy the toys.
3. 40 – 9.95 – 9.95 – 12.63 = 7.47
His change is $7.47.
4. (21.65 – 12.99) + (21.65 – 12.99) = 17.32
He will save $17.32.

B. 1. More probable
2. Less probable
3. Equally probable

C. 1.

2.

D. 1. $\frac{2}{10}$; 2
2. $\frac{1}{10}$; 1 tenth
3. $\frac{4}{10}$; 4 tenths
4. $\frac{3}{10}$; 3 tenths

E. 1. Wilson
2. Ryan
3. a. 396 g
b. 198 g
c. 792 g
d. 594 g
4. No

F. 1. A 2. B

Brain Teaser

19

English

A. 1. Mia would walk off the field if a game was not going her way.
2. A university scout recognized her talent and recruited her to the team.
3. (Individual answer)

B. 1. O 2. F
3. F 4. O
5. F 6. F
7. O

C. 1. Tree
2. Flowers
3. Baseball Game
4. Movies
5. Pets
6. Book
7. Family
8. Happy
9. Fruit
10. Sports
11. Small
12. Jobs

D. (Individual writing)

Science

A. 1. E 2. B 3. A
4. C 5. D

B.

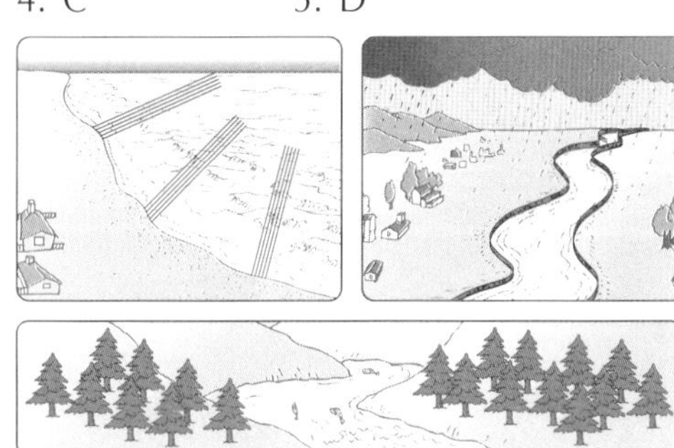

C. 1. flood
2. landslide
3. tornado
4. earthquake
5. storm

D. (Individual observation)

Social Studies

1. Ledge
2. Arrow loop
3. Wall
4. Drawbridge
5. Moat
6. Catapult

Week 7

Mathematics

A. 1.
```
    1 3 8
4 ) 5 5 2
    4
    1 5
    1 2
      3 2
      3 2
```
138

2.
```
    1 5 9
5 ) 7 9 5
    5
    2 9
    2 5
      4 5
      4 5
```
159

3.
```
      9 1
9 ) 8 1 9
    8 1
        9
        9
```
91

4.
```
    1 2 4
6 ) 7 4 4
    6
    1 4
    1 2
      2 4
      2 4
```
124

5.
```
      8 7
8 ) 6 9 6
    6 4
      5 6
      5 6
```
87

6.

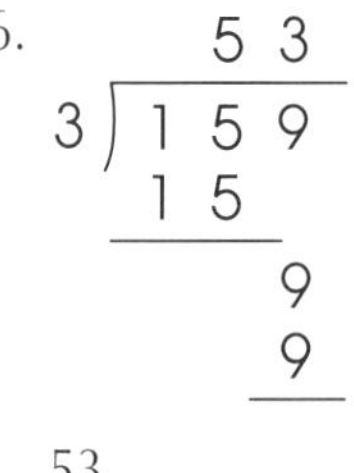

```
      5 3
3 ) 1 5 9
    1 5
        9
        9
```
53

B. 1. Cylinder
2. Rectangular pyramid
3. Rectangular prism
4. Triangular prism

C. Sun : 4968 ; 5000
Mon : 3006 ; 3000
Tue : 2481 ; 2500
Wed : 3459 ; 3500
Thu : 2963 ; 3000
Fri : 3977 ; 4000
Sat : 5483 ; 5500

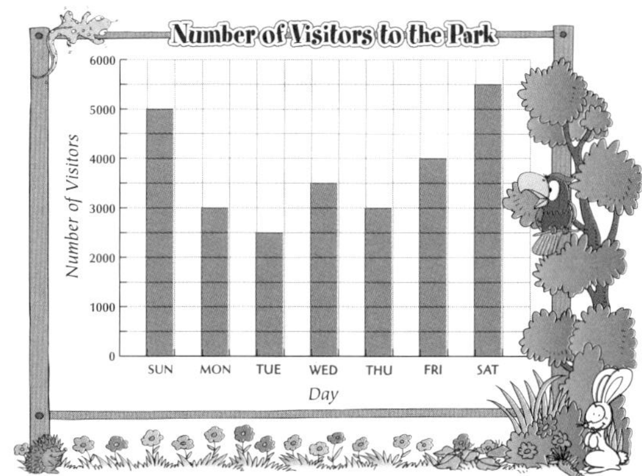

D. 1. Number of Visitors to the Park
2. Number of Visitors
3. Day
4. From 0 to 6000
5. 1000
6. Sunday, Friday, and Saturday

Brain Teaser

4126

English

A. 1. During Mayan times, if a team lost, a human sacrifice was performed.
2. Over 600 ball courts have been found in Mexico by archaeologists.

3. They wore fine jewellery, animal skins, and feathered headdresses.
4. They had to keep the ball in the air.
5. The game ball was made from a human skull wrapped with strips of rubber from the native rubber tree.
6. They believed that by playing this game correctly, the gods would provide bountiful crops and good health for their people.

B. 1. In a Pok-a-Tok ball court, there are three round disks on the two sloping walls.
2. The Pok-a-Tok players wore protective gear during the game to allow for quick movement.
3. A human sacrifice would be performed by killing the captain or coach of the losing team.

C.

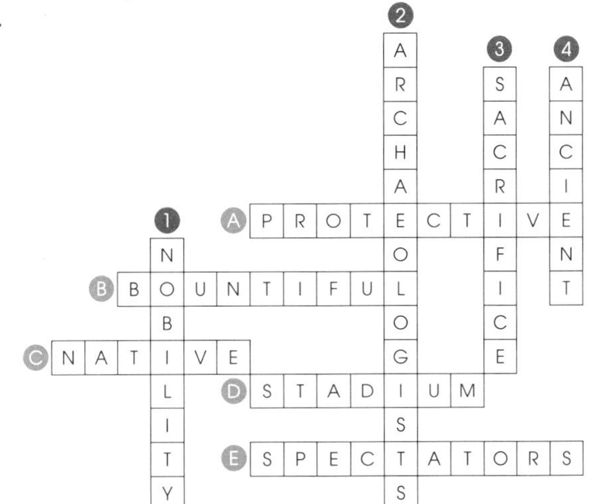

D. (Individual lists)
E. (Individual writing)

Science

A. 1. Nervous
2. Brain
3. Digestive
4. Stomach
5. Skeletal
6. Bone
7. Excretory
8. Kidney
9. Circulatory
10. Heart
11. Respiratory
12. Lung

B.

h	m	d	y	c	y	s	k	s	r
t	l	u	o	e	p	m	u	l	s
u	n	r	s	i	n	g	x	e	e
o	d	e	n	c	a	d	n	h	t
m	i	a	r	h	l	o	i	l	r
a	l	l	p	v	b	e	y	k	a
e	s	o	n	r	e	o	s	p	c
i	s	y	r	e	t	r	a	c	h
e	i	n	t	e	s	t	i	n	e
s	k	u	l	l	p	q	y	j	a

Social Studies

A. 1. Before
2. Before
3. Before
4. After
5. After
6. After
7. After
8. After
9. After
10. Before

B. 1. then
2. now
3. both
4. then
5. then
6. both
7. now
8. then
9. both
10. then
11. both
12. then

Week 8

Mathematics

A. 1.

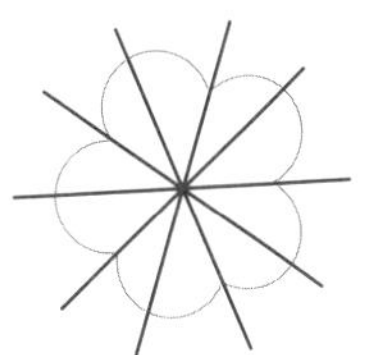

2.

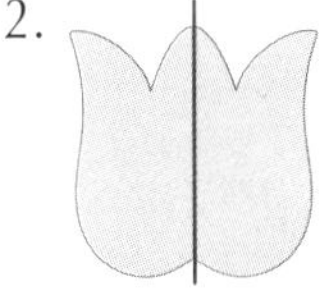

3.

4.

5.

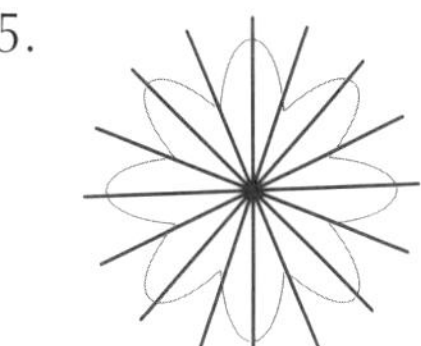

6.

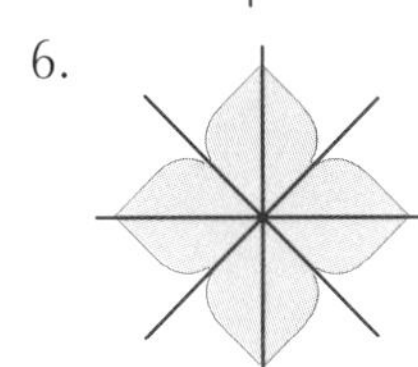

B. 1. A : 40° ; B : 65° ; C : 30° ; D : 115°
   2. 231 ÷ 5 = 46R1 ; 46
   3. 85 ÷ 8 = 10R5 ; 10
   4. 108 x 2 = 216 ; 216

C. 1. Mabel : 57
   Ivy : 43
   Winnie : 49
   Stella : 64
   2. Stella
   3. Ivy
   4. 4:02

D. 1. C   2. A   3. A

Math Game

1

English

A. (Suggested answers)
   1. Playing baseball
   2. Rollerblading
   3. Seeing snow

B. (Individual writing)

C.

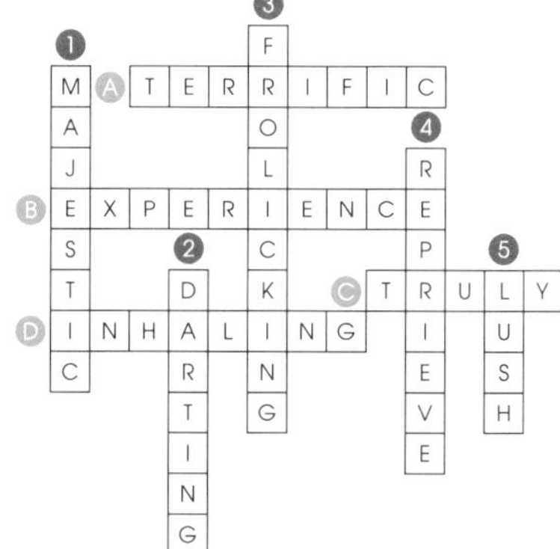

D. 1. ugly
   2. stale
   3. tiny
   4. cold
   5. last
   6. leave
   7. inside
   8. stranger

E. 1. lush ; bloom ; walks
   2. hot ; shade ; Running
   3. shades ; frolicking ; pile

Science

A. 1. climate   2. weather
   3. weather   4. climate
   5. weather   6. climate
   7. climate   8. climate

B.

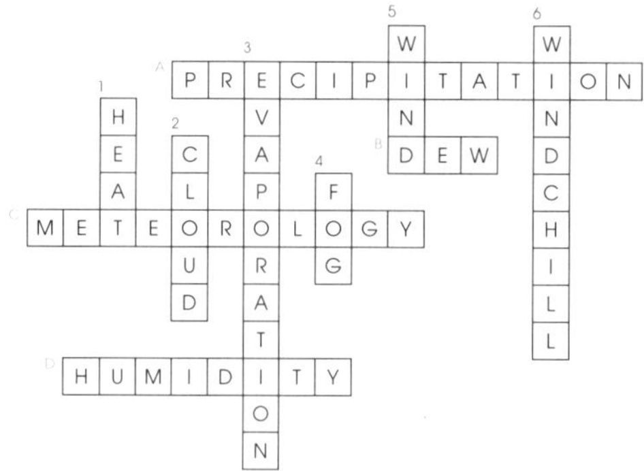

Social Studies

A. 1. B   2. C
   3. B   4. A
   5. B   6. A
   7. C   8. C

B. Stonemason : A
   Stone and Wood Carver : D, G, H
   Glass Worker : C, F
   Carpenter : B, E

My 3-D Calendar

Write something to remind yourself in the spaces provided. Then cut out the net and glue the prism.

Saturday is for ____.

Monday is for ____.

Tuesday is for ____.

Wednesday is for ____.

Thursday is for ____.

Friday is for ____.

Sunday is for ____.

Glue

I Love Sandwiches

Cut and glue the triangular prisms to make your delicious sandwich. Cut out the napkin and the tag. Then write the name of someone special on the tag.

MOM'S SANDWICH

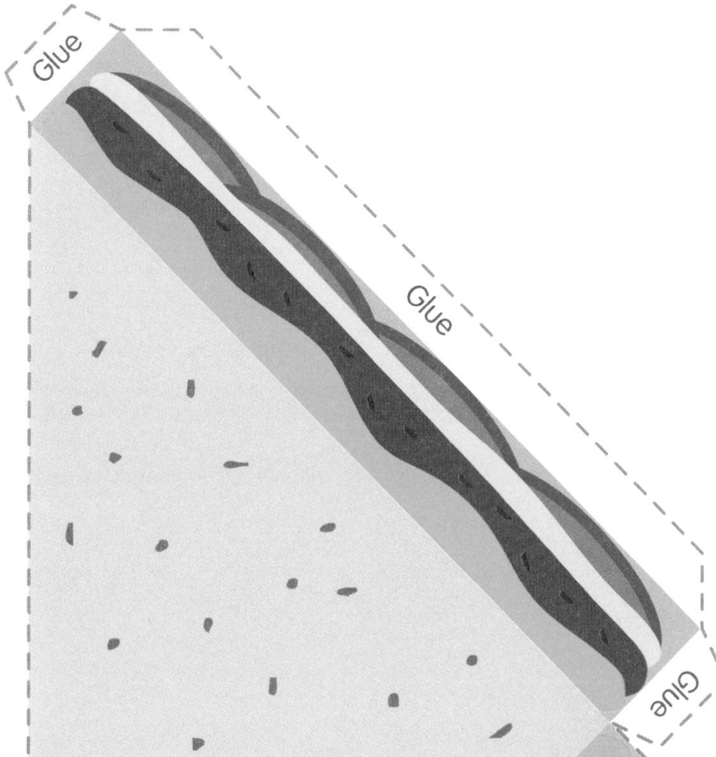

Glue

Glue

Glue

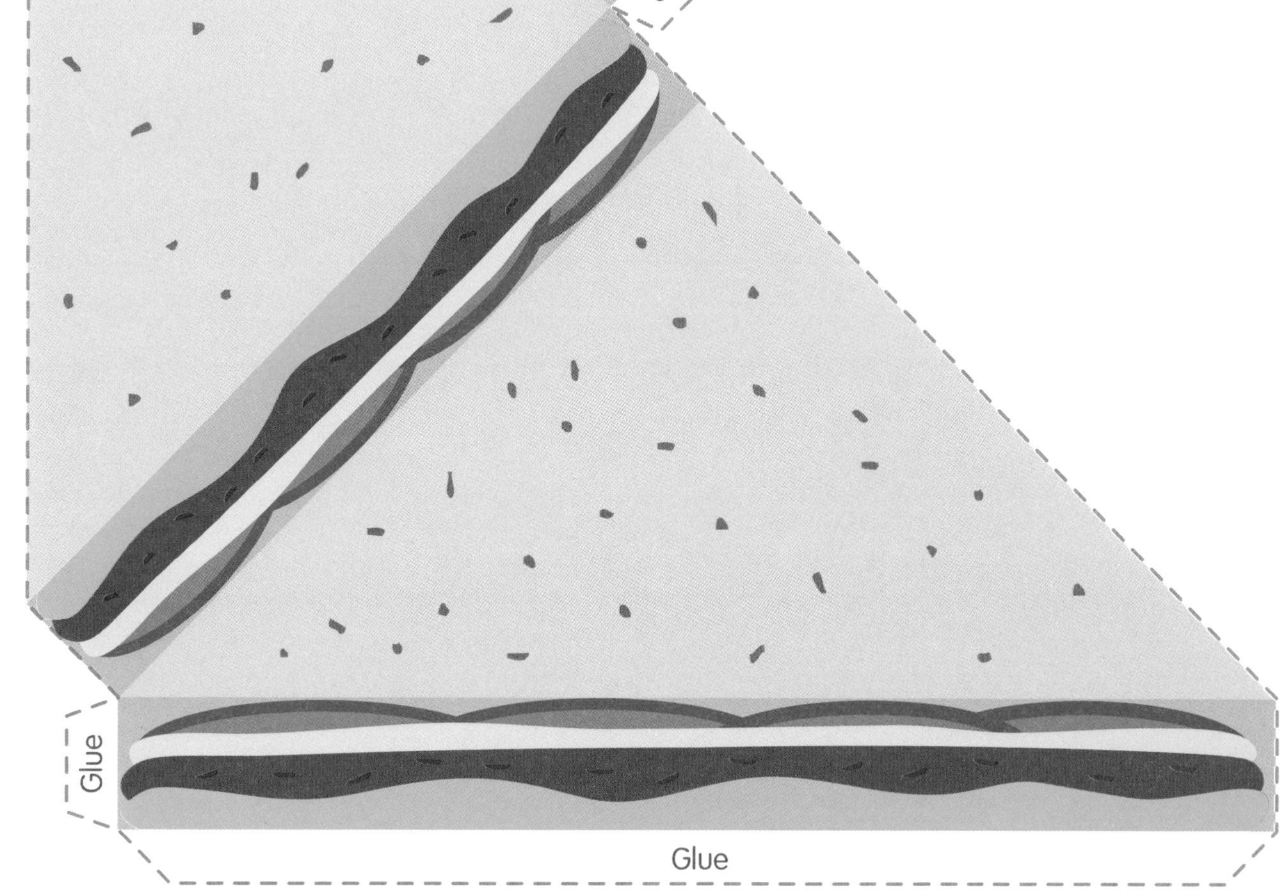

Glue

Glue

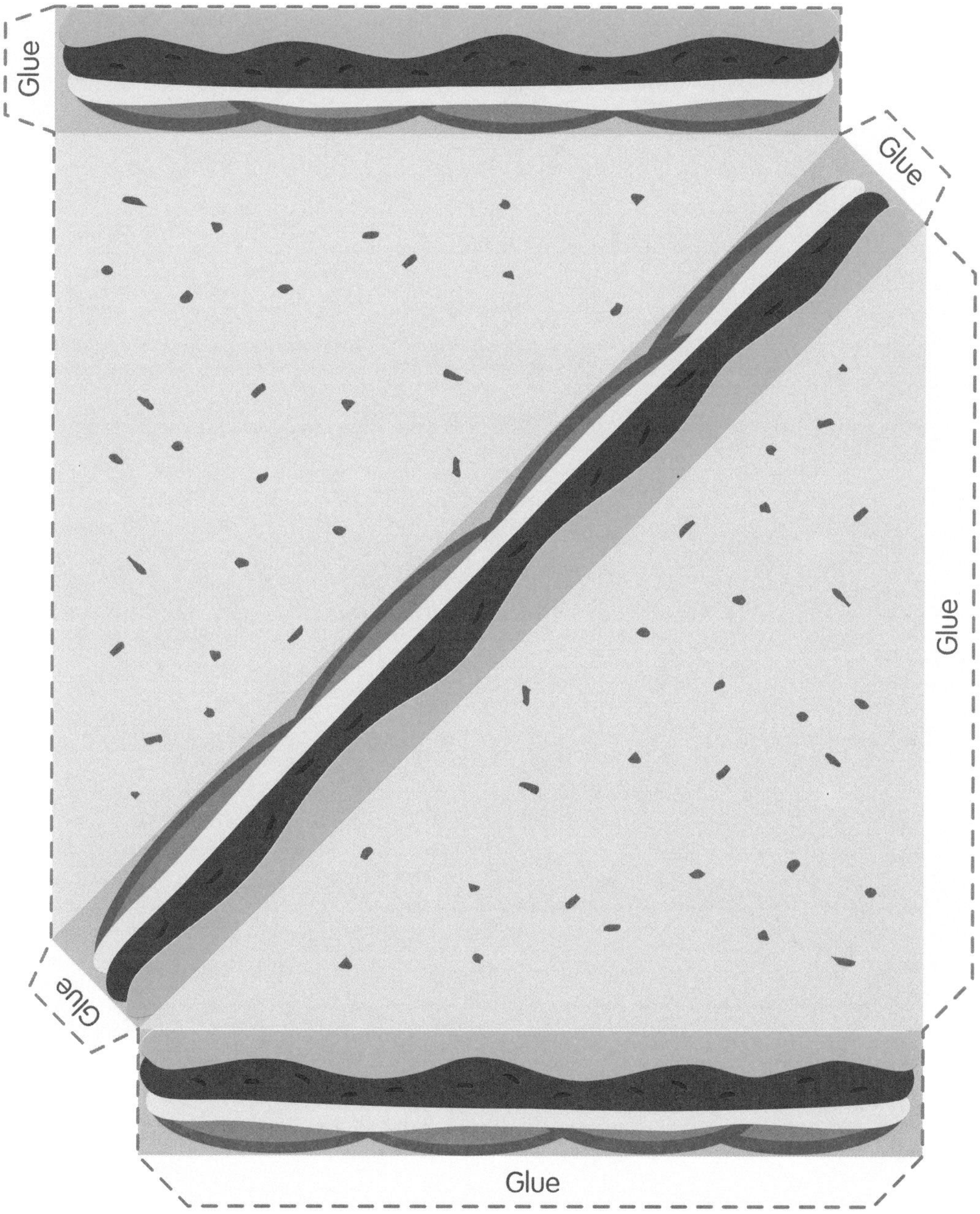

Glue

Glue

Glue

Glue

Glue

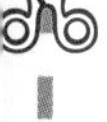

napkin

An Angel Messenger

Cut out the angel and the message sheets. Give the sheets to your parents, teachers, or friends and ask them to write you something encouraging. Staple the messages together.

Poke holes here and tie a string.
Then hang up the angel.

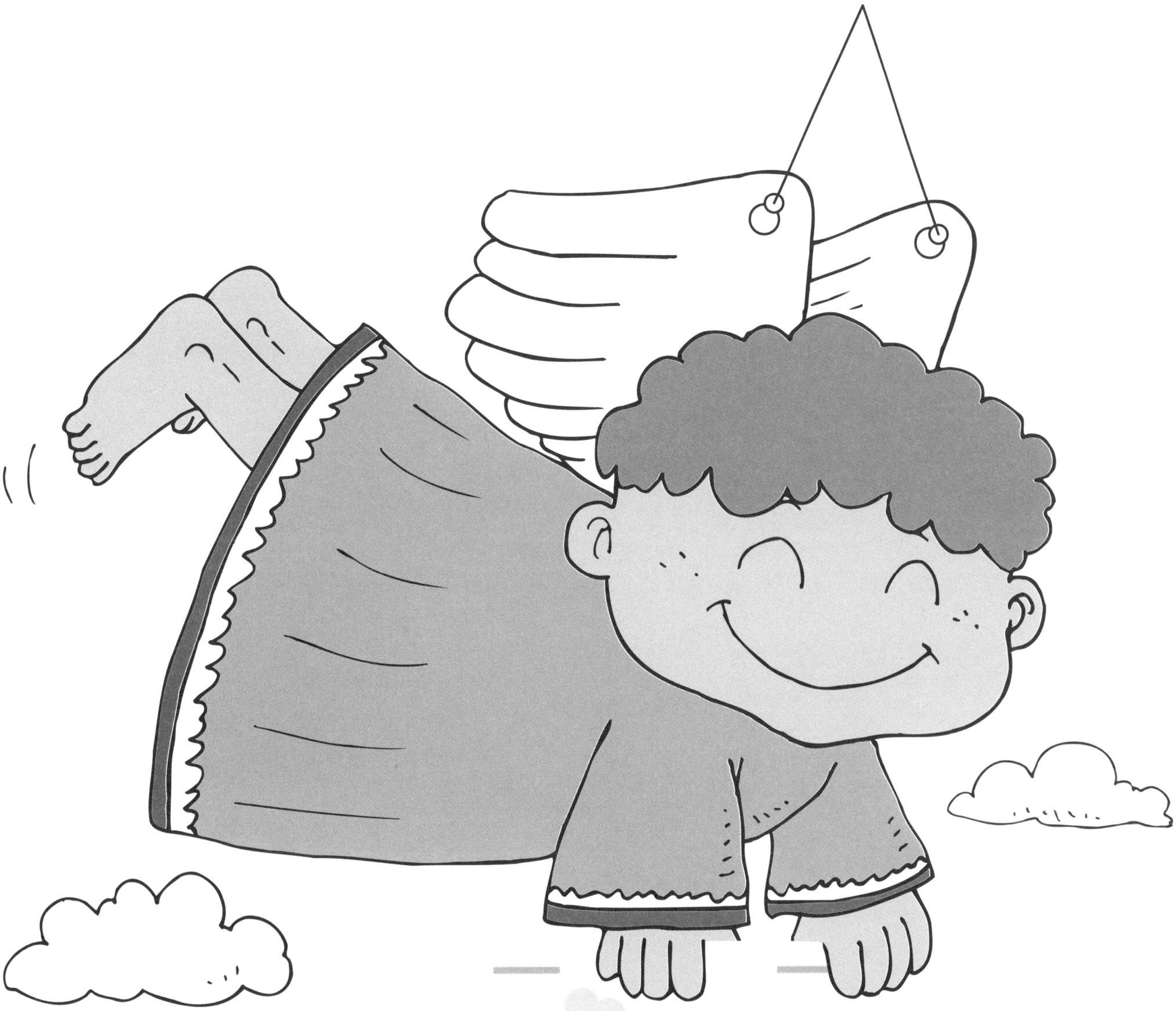

Messages from My
Beloved Ones

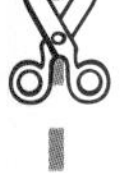

HANDS-ON

My New Word Collection

Cut out the root words, prefixes, and suffixes. Then match the correct pieces to form new words.

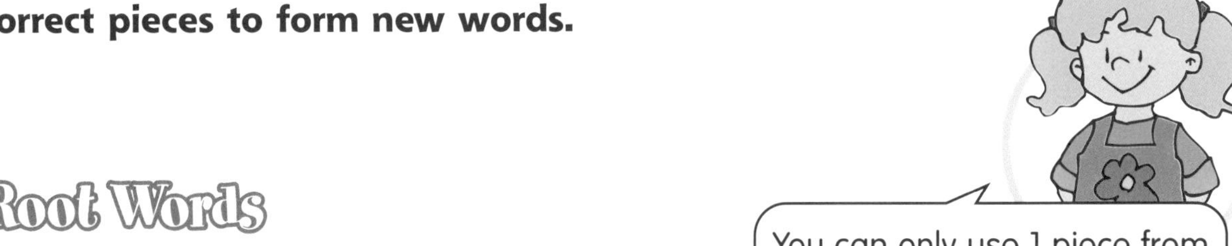

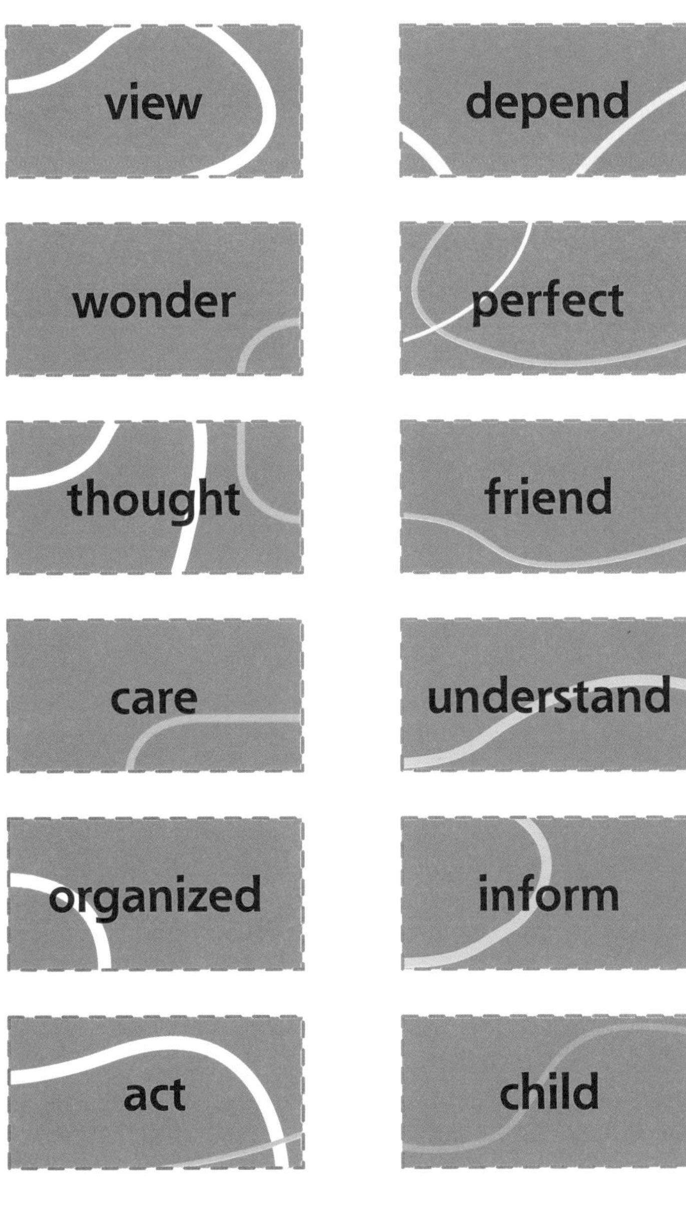

Prefixes

in

dis

mis

pre

im

re

Suffixes

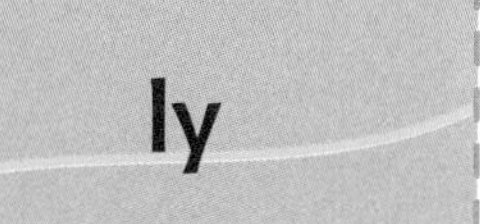

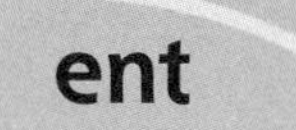

You should be able to make 29 words in all. Answers are at the back of this page.

Answers:

wonderful
independent
childlike
friendly
rethought
disorganized
misunderstand
active
reaction
inactive
inspection
review
perfection
imperfect
imperfectly
dependent
childish
redness
thoughtful
reorganized
careful
action
react
inaction
inspect
misinform
preview
perfectly
imperfection

My Picture Poem

Cut out the pictures and place them over the boxes to complete the poem. You can mix and match the pictures as long as the poem makes sense.

My ☐

With a ☐ in hand

Wearing ☐

Hair blown over the ☐

Slouching slightly

Standing under a ☐

Away from the ☐

A sign of old age, perhaps

But feeling at ☐